BEAGLING

The Sports and Pastimes Library

DINGHY AND SMALL CLASS RACING
By T. Norman Hinton.   10s. 6d. net.

THE ART OF SALMON FISHING
By Jock Scott.   10s. 6d. net.

THE ART OF FLY FISHING
By Lieut.-Col. W. Keith Rollo.   10s. 6d. net

THE ART OF COARSE FISHING
By J. H. R. Bazley.   8s. 6d. net.

THE ART OF SHOOTING AND ROUGH SHOOT MANAGEMENT
By Leslie Sprake.   10s. 6d. net.

BEAGLING
By Captain J. Otho Paget.   10s. 6d. net.

THE ART OF MOUNTAIN TRAMPING
By Richard W. Hall.   8s. 6d. net.

THE ART OF CAMPING
By W. T. Palmer.   8s. 6d. net.

THE ART OF DOG TRAINING
By Leslie Sprake.   8s. 6d. net.

THE ART OF BIRD WATCHING
By E. M. Nicholson.   10s. 6d. net.

THE ART OF FENCING
By R. A. Lidstone.   10s. 6d. net.

THE ART OF CROQUET
By H. F. Crowther-Smith.   10s. 6d. net.

THE ART OF BOWLS
By Felix Hotchkiss.   10s. 6d. net.

SAILING
By Major-General H. J. K. Bamfield, C.B., and S. E. Palmer.   10s. 6d. net.

THE ART OF LAKE FISHING (WITH SUNK FLY)
By Sidney Spencer.   10s. 6d. net.

(Frontispiece) MOVING OFF TO DRAW

BEAGLING

A PRACTICAL HANDBOOK ON THE
SPORT AND KENNEL MANAGEMENT

By
Captain J. OTHO PAGET

*WITH PHOTOGRAPHS AND DIAGRAMS;
AND TEXT SKETCHES BY*
T. IVESTER LLOYD

The
Sports and Pastimes
Library

H. F. & G. WITHERBY LTD.
326 · HIGH HOLBORN · LONDON · W.C.

First published under the title
"THE ART OF BEAGLING"
1931

Second impression under the title
"BEAGLING" - 1938

Printed for Messrs. H. F. & G. Witherby Ltd.
by J. & J. Gray, Edinburgh

PREFACE

A SPORT FOR ALL

MONEY is very useful at times and all think that however much is in our pocket we should be happier with a little more.

Riches are no aid to happiness without good health—a truism everyone will admit, and yet a fact often forgotten in the daily scramble to attain more wealth.

Labour, whether physical or mental, is the greatest factor towards the making of a full and contented life, but all work and no play robs existence of the sparkle of joy, which helps to brighten the dreary days of gloom.

A judicious allocation of days for recreation is necessary for everyone's welfare and there is nothing better than the chase.

Riding to foxhounds may be beyond the means of many people, but the outlay, including a small subscription, to follow a pack of foot-beagles should not be a heavy burden on a lightly filled purse.

PREFACE

A day with beagles means fresh air and exercise with the additional pleasure of listening to the music of hounds. In the majority of people the cry of hounds awakes a feeling of enthusiasm which is difficult to explain and induces them to follow as best they can.

Even with foxhounds men and women will start to run in pursuit, though they know the pack will be out of sight in a few minutes, but the desire is there.

With a large percentage of the population love of the chase is a hereditary instinct, but of course many of those who have passed their lives in towns are not conscious they possess it. Let them go out two or three days with beagles and they will soon find the hunting fever has only been hidden by the absence of opportunity.

Besides those who have to work for a living, there are many young men not interested in the art of riding, or accustomed to country pursuits, who for want of healthy exercise and occupation develop all the vices Satan finds for the idle. This is another class that would be all the better physically and mentally for following beagles.

It has been the custom for many years for " highbrows " to scoff at the sport of hunting and those who live in the country. Because a man has

PREFACE

certain literary attainments, and is able to express himself lucidly, it does not give him the right to condemn a sport with the details of which he is totally ignorant. Most of these men work and spend their lives in crowded cities, with a visit to a club for recreation. Neglecting their bodily welfare in working the brain they are incapable of producing a healthy race of children. They also fail to pass on the brain power they themselves possess.

Men of great intellect who have neglected the wants of the body very seldom produce worthy descendants. The race of town-dwellers would soon die out were it not for the constant infusion of fresh blood from the country.

The last word will never be written on hunting subjects, and though these pages do not pretend to cover every detail, the novice will find hints that may be useful to him both in kennel and field.

J. O. P.

CONTENTS

CHAPTER	PAGE
PREFACE	7
I. INTRODUCTION	17
II. THE HOUND—	
Height	21
Reasons for Height	22
Looks	26
Large and Small Hounds	26
Legs and Shoulders	28
Back, Loin, Quarters, and Hip	31
Feet	33
Nose	37
Character and Expression	38
Purchase, Prices and Luck	40
Peterborough	44
A Comparison	45
Showing Hints	45
III. BROOD BITCHES, WHELPS, AND YOUNG HOUNDS—	
Whelping	49
Litter Feeding	51
Exercising Space	53
Doctoring	55
Walking	56
Marking and Recording	59
Walking Prizes and Entertainment	61
IV. ON BREEDING—	
Picked Bitches	64
Qualities of the Sire	66
Balance	67
Quality and Looks	68
Babblers and Skirters	69
The Mute Hound	71
Period of Vitality	72

CONTENTS

Inbreeding 73
Best Time for Birth 78
Dosing 79

V. KENNELS AND KENNEL MANAGEMENT—
Ventilation 81
Brick v. Wood 83
Kennel Lameness and Floor Ventilation . . . 83
Roof and Windows 86
Yard Spaces and Aspect 86
Drain-traps 88
Accommodation and Overcrowding 89
General Design and Details 89
Feeding 91
Change of Diet 92
Feeding Times 96
Appetites 97
Summer Exercise and Condition 98
Discipline 102
Medicine and Dipping 103

VI. THE KENNELMAN—
Kennelman-cum-Whip 110
Disposition and Experience 111
Age 112
Housing 114
Duties 115

VII. DISEASES—
Distemper and Treatment 116
Jaundice 121
Chorea 121
Hysteria, Possible Causes and Treatment . . . 126

VIII. THE HARE—
Pugnacity and Nerve 135
Tricks and Stamina 138
Wild and Semi-Tame 141
Preservation 143
Marital Relations 145
Leverets 146
Tricks 148

IX. THE COUNTRY—
Neighbouring Hunts, Owners and Tenants . . 152

CONTENTS

    Scratch Packs 155
    Ownership 157
    Nomenclature 159

X. THE HUNTSMAN AND HUNTING—
    Advice in the Field 161
    Hallooing and Signals 163
    Hunting Methods 164
    The Kill 167
    Recovering the Line 169
    Picking out a Scent 169
    Tricks of a Tired Hare 170
    Casting and Lifting 171
    Decisions and Conditions 175
    Perseverance 181
    Heads up 181

XI. THE WHIPPER-IN—
    Obedience to the Huntsman 183
    Carrying a Whip 184
    Counting the Pack 185
    Position 186
    Damage to Property 188
    Stopping Riot 190
    Rating 192
    The Noisy Whip 194
    Exercising 197
    The Young Hound 197

XII. THE FIELD—
    Subscription and Ownership of Packs . . . 201
    Hunt Uniform 205
    Followers' Kit 205
    Importance of Footwear 206
    Consideration and Care against Damage . . . 209
    Fitness 211
    Hound-Pace and Man-Pace 211
    Human Scent 213
    Position 213
    Hound Identification 214
    Rules to Follow in the Field 214
    Sympathy with the Hound 217

INDEX 219

LIST OF ILLUSTRATIONS

PLATES

Moving off to Draw		*Frontispiece*
A Fourteen-inch Pack		*facing page* 32
A Little Air and Exercise		,, ,, 54
A Fine Litter		,, ,, 54
Ready for the Fray—A Fourteen-inch Pack in the Kennel Yard		,, ,, 88
Transported from Kennel to Meet by Light Motor Car Trailer		,, ,, 88
Over the Plough		,, ,, 156
Out of the Stubble into the Roots		,, ,, 156
Down in the Marsh Land		,, ,, 156
Drawing up to the Hare over Meadowland		,, ,, 170
Lifting Hounds on to the Hare		,, ,, 170
Drawing in the Rough		,, ,, 170
Casting over Plough		,, ,, 170
The Kill		,, ,, 180
The Worry		,, ,, 180
The Hunt in Progress, showing Correct Position of Whips and Field		,, ,, 214
Through the Roots		,, ,, 214
Changing Ground		,, ,, 214
A Water Obstacle		,, ,, 214

LIST OF ILLUSTRATIONS

DIAGRAMS AND TEXT FIGURES

KENNEL, FRONT AND SIDE ELEVATION	*page* 84
KENNEL AND YARD, GROUND PLAN	,, 87
FRESH	,, 136
FIRST ALARM	,, 139
LISTENING	,, 143
LAST EFFORT	,, 148
DEAD BEAT	,, 150
IN FULL CRY	,, 168
METHOD OF CASTING AT CHECK	,, 173

CHAPTER I

INTRODUCTION

THE increasing popularity attending the pursuit of the hare is merely a revival of the chase in its oldest form. The wild hare of ancient days was held in great honour; an animal that would bring out the best qualities of hounds and huntsman to pursue it to a kill. At that period the fox was held in small esteem; an outlaw to be captured by any means, and no one cared how he was " trapped or slain."

In addition to the actual sport of hunting, the delirious excitement of riding across country after hounds became appreciated, and in consequence the fox rose at once to his high estate. About the same time when much of the land was enclosed, and many landlords wished to increase their head of game, the system of preservation came into vogue. This would have been well enough if not carried to excess, but in countries with a suitable soil and abundant feeding ground, hares quickly multiplied and were a nuisance to the occupier.

THE ART OF BEAGLING

Up to then the wild hare had only survived from pursuit by men and dogs by the exercise of all her cunning. With the protection from her natural enemies she soon became a semi-tame animal, wandering about the fields in droves, naked and unashamed before the eye of man. Generations of inherited instincts were thus temporarily obscured, and the wild character of the animal lost.

The desire of indifferent shots to massacre wholesale, and to see the results of their prowess recorded in the Press, may have led to the excessive preservation of the hare. It is difficult to understand the mentality of men with the ability to hit a haystack finding any sport in shooting at such an easy target; and still more strange that they should care to continue the slaughter. The Hares and Rabbits Bill, however, put that sport out of fashion, except in specially favoured districts, so that the hare had once more to fall back on her natural cunning to avoid extinction, and the survivors regained the wild attributes of distant forbears.

In countries where preservation was almost unknown, the hare not having been pampered or allowed unnatural ease, retained all those inherited qualities which enabled her ancestors

INTRODUCTION

in bygone days to defeat the craft of hounds and huntsman.

The fox has many and various tricks up his sleeve, but they are nothing compared to the numerous artifices of the hare. Truly she is a beast of the chase it is a pleasure to hunt, and, unless out-paced at the start by too big hounds, may always be depended upon to put up a good fight.

There is a widespread idea that the hare is a very timorous animal, whereas she is really very bold, and except when weak, or wounded, is well able to take care of herself. No fox will ever attack a healthy hare, and if attempting it once will not be likely to try a second time. What has led to the hare being considered timid is her very highly strung nervous system, which is controlled by an exceptionally acute sense of hearing and smell.

Those who have witnessed fights between jack hares in the spring of the year can testify to their pugnacity, and it is by no means uncommon to pick up carcasses of the vanquished after a battle.

Although it is impossible to enter into the exact feelings of a hunted hare, my own opinion is that up to almost the last moment she always expects to escape by her natural cunning.

THE ART OF BEAGLING

When fox-hunting is impossible and the inhabitants of the district want to ride, harriers afford a pleasant makeshift, but in order to see the finer shades of venerie a hare should be hunted with small hounds, and the followers, including the huntsman, should all be afoot.

A pack of beagles, preferably under fifteen inches, will give those who follow good exercise and the best of sport. Exercise of some kind is essential to health, and hunting is the form prescribed by nature. Whatever recreation we indulge in should be sufficiently engrossing to absorb our whole interest and attention. Otherwise the muscles may automatically be put in play, but unless they are working in conjunction with the brain neither will derive the full benefit. The business or professional man devoting his whole time to a sedentary occupation is liable to a nervous breakdown by overtaxing the mind and neglecting the body, so that any sport or pastime he takes up should be of a character to relieve all mental strain, and allow him temporarily to forget life's worries.

CHAPTER II

THE HOUND

Height—Reasons for Height—Look—Large and Small Hounds—Legs and Shoulders—Back, Loin, Quarters and Hip—Feet—Nose—Character and Expression—Purchase, Prices and Luck—Peterborough—A Comparison—Showing Hints.

HEIGHT

THE height of the beagle must be determined to a certain extent by the country over which it is intended to hunt. As there are numerous ditches in the Fens, and with sometimes steep cut banks, a hound less than 14 inches is at a great disadvantage and is likely to be tired before the hare. A country consisting chiefly of heavy plough also requires larger hounds, but it must be remembered a hare is greatly handicapped in sticky " going " as her pads quickly get clogged with mud. A 13-inch pack, when properly fit, ought to be able to account for their hares even if they never cross a grass field. Perhaps the most trying ordeal for the small hound is to be running all day in root crops, the tops of which are usually wet and above his shoulders, so that back and loins are soaked

THE ART OF BEAGLING

with no chance of getting dry. With the weather moderately warm, as is often the case in the autumn, this does not much matter, but a cold day with an east wind, when the undercoat becomes thoroughly sodden, a few hours under those conditions chills the body and lowers the vitality.

REASONS FOR HEIGHT

The fastest runner cannot hope to keep up with even an under 13-inch pack when scent is really good, but naturally they can be nearer them than with larger hounds. The chief objection to the 16-inch hound is that he goes faster when only hunting a cold scent than the average man can maintain for any time, and thus the pleasure of watching hounds hunt is missed. My reason for disliking 16-inch packs is that the huntsman very seldom has the opportunity of ascertaining which are only average hounds, and which have extra good noses. It is easier with these big hounds to find a fresh hare, and starting off on good terms, catch her in thirty-five or forty minutes, rather than to continue persevering on a cold line. This procedure may be more satisfactory to the younger members of the field, but it does not bring out the finer qualities of individual hounds and tends in

THE HOUND

course of time to ruin the pack. Patience, perseverance, and the ability to remain steadfast to the line of the hunted animal are essential to a beagle, or as a matter of fact, to any other hound.

The ideal size for hare-hunting beagles followed on foot is $14\frac{1}{2}$ inches. Hounds of this size will be found suitable for every description of country and, if good enough, will show sport as well as catch their hares. Thirteen-inch hounds allow followers to see more hunting, and when in a country where they can account for their hares fairly often, they should be preferred. A hare can go very nearly as fast for a short distance, almost up to the moment when her strength fails, as when she first started from her form, so that a pack of small hounds gets very little advantage from a view. The bigger hounds on getting a view of the hunted hare are generally able to keep her in sight and course her down.

Everyone endeavours to get his hounds as near as possible of the same height, but size matters very little, and the important point is to get them of the same pace. It may be very annoying to have to draft your best hound, but if he is too fast for the others it is only ruining the pack to keep him. A ruthless " heading and tailing " is necessary if you would have your pack run as if covered by the proverbial sheet, and unless they do that you cannot expect good results.

The reason of this is obvious when a little common sense is used in thinking the matter out. A hound faster than the others and with a fairly good nose is able to keep its comrades at full stretch without allowing them to get a whiff of the scent, so that they take no part in the hunt. When it comes to slow hunting then is their opportunity for joining in, but having previously only followed a leader without the assistance of scent, they are at a considerable disadvantage on getting their heads down. One hound, however good he may be, is pretty certain on the best scenting day to be at fault sooner or later, and by the time the others come up, many valuable minutes are lost before the line is recovered. The pace of a run as far as the hare is concerned, depends not on the speed hounds may go at intervals, but on the continuity of their running without checks; in fact it is the moral taught by the old hare and tortoise fable. A good pack evenly matched in pace and with no sleeping partners will hardly lose a second at a check, and in consequence never give a hare the opportunity of regaining her wind. The hare's speed and lung power are exceptionally good for some distance,

THE HOUND

as witness her frequent escape from greyhounds, but if she is never allowed to rest a moment she soon becomes exhausted.

Here is an illustration of my meaning, and though I do not pretend to know the actual rate hounds run, the difference between eight and twelve miles an hour should represent the difference between packs of 13 and 15 inches. We will suppose the run is 12 miles and that a pack of 15 inches, though ill-matched for speed, run when on a scent at the rate of 12 miles an hour. Without checks it would, of course, accomplish the distance in an hour, but unless there was breast high scent its unevenness would cause numerous stoppages, and we can safely say there would be eight checks, each lasting at least five minutes, so that instead of an hour the time would be actually an hour and 40 minutes. The perfectly matched 13-inch pack, running at only eight miles an hour, but without a check, would complete the run in 10 minutes less than the bigger hounds. Five minutes is in reality a very low estimate of the time lost at a check, both with beagles and foxhounds.

I dislike hearing of a master who intends to increase the height of his pack, because it usually means he is dissatisfied with his hounds, and they are not accounting for their hares. It should be

THE ART OF BEAGLING

the chief ambition of every breeder or owner to improve the hunting abilities of his pack, and then, with their rise, to gradually lower his standard.

LOOKS

The very laudable desire of most masters to have a good-looking pack is often a reason for keeping the bigger sort, as it cannot be denied the best-looking are more often above 15 inches than under.

After all, the size of the hounds a man intends to hunt with is a personal matter in which he must be allowed to choose the height he considers most suitable. There are packs well up to the 16-inch limit, and I would not presume to say that those who fancy them are wrong, but it seems to me the pleasure of following beagles on foot is in being able to see them hunt, and naturally the bigger they are the less they can be seen. Then, when the huntsman wants to lift or cast these large hounds, he is unable to run fast enough to keep them moving at a pace which co-ordinates with their natural speed.

LARGE AND SMALL HOUNDS

The real reason for having large hounds is that hares are easier to catch, but the smaller the hounds

THE HOUND

the greater the test of hunting capacity, and the greater the triumph when the hare is caught. My own idea has always been to measure the pace of beagles in hunting a hare with that of foxhounds hunting a fox, and try to make the odds practically the same.

In setting out to improve the appearance of a pack, breeders should be very careful how they proceed to attain that end, and always bear in mind that the real test is the hunting field. Beagle men have followed in the footsteps of foxhound breeders, and are liable to make the same mistakes, to sacrifice super-excellent hunting qualities on the altar of fashion. The straight front legs and the Belvoir tan are very pleasing to the eye, but unless accompanied by good scenting powers, courage and stamina, they are of little use to a hound meant for hunting. Shoulders, quarters, ribs, and balance are the essential qualities in the conformation of a hound, but perhaps the sloping shoulder is the most important. Colour is immaterial, but the badger-pie and other light colours, now rather out of fashion, usually indicate extra good hunting ability. Why then should we try to rule them out?

Peterborough is now the only show patronised by genuine hare-hunting packs, and with this one occasion to exhibit their hounds it might be thought masters would not allow the decisions arrived at there to influence them.

I rather fear that the show does more harm than good in that breeders think more of producing a hound to win prizes, than one that will be perfect in the hunting field. The ribbons that decorate the coats of fortunate kennelmen at the show do not by any means indicate the pack's ability to hunt a hare to death. The chief benefit derived from the show is that it enables a man to compare his hounds with others, and for that reason it would be well for everyone to show what he considers his best, even with no chance of winning a prize. The unsuccessful exhibitor should not be downhearted and inclined to scrap an animal because it has not pleased the judges, but has proved by its performance in the field to have nothing wrong with its conformation.

Judges have to make their decisions on certain accepted lines and, unless they adhere in the main to them, the results of shows would be chaos and no one would know what to exhibit.

LEGS AND SHOULDERS

In the early days of Peterborough, the straight front legs were very rare, and with the object of im-

THE HOUND

proving the breed in that direction, straightness was made the chief point. The crooked Basset-like forelegs would undoubtedly result from breeding from hounds with that defect, and would be accentuated in succeeding generations. Few hounds are shown nowadays that are really crooked, so that Peterborough has justified its existence in one particular.

A man need not be a good judge to tell whether a hound stands straight on the flags, but standing straight does not always mean moving straight, and one which appears plumb when facing the judges, may be badly out at the elbows.

To be tied in at the elbows is perhaps worse, but both are faults that restrict the free movement of legs.

Shoulders, which I have said are the most important point in a hound's conformation, are very difficult to see and be certain about in the restricted area of a ring. The only real test is to watch the hound galloping at full speed over rough ground, but as that is impossible at a show we have to do the best we can under the circumstances. The old fallacy that a long neck meant good shoulders has been exploded, and though the graceful, swanlike neck may influence a judge in his decision it is no guarantee of a sloping shoulder. The point at the shoulder-blade where it touches the back should be behind the elbow, or at least not in front of it. This is the secret of good or bad shoulders, but it is very difficult to ascertain this with a hound that is loaded with fat.

Let us return for a moment to the straight leg subject. Our foxhound brethren set us the example of improving their hounds in that respect, and in the laudable desire to attain perfection may have rather overdone it, thereby creating an unnatural formation, out of harmony with the rest of the body. In fact, it is only within the last year or two that foxhound breeders have come to realise that the knuckling over at the knee, which had been considered the acme of straightness, was a deformity. A slight bend backwards at the knee is still considered a fault, and it may be presumption to disagree with acknowledged authorities, but there are many more hounds lamed every season from being straight from knee to foot than those that are back at the knee. The knee of a hound, as far as his movements are concerned, is much the same as a horse's fetlock, and the latter's pastern is relatively the same as knee to foot in a hound. We know that too much slope in a horse's pastern and too much length is a weakness, but we also know that when short and upright they are unlikely to stand hard work.

THE HOUND

When either horse or hound is going at top speed he must naturally hit the ground with great force, and it stands to reason that if the leg is practically in a straight line both shoulders and body will receive the whole jar. A kennel that is frequently handicapped with having to leave hounds at home through lameness caused by shaken shoulders, injured feet, and other like ailments, would do well to think the matter out.

BACK, LOIN AND QUARTERS

There is an undoubted tendency to pay more attention to the forward than to the hind quarters and a hound that presents a pleasing front to the judges is often forgiven deficiencies behind. Back, loin, quarters, and the length from hip to hock are the chief factors in the driving power which enables a hound not only to go fast, but to keep on going without the effort that tires. Fairly wide quarters are to be preferred, but it happens occasionally that when a hound is somewhat narrow he has exceptionally long second thighs, and is correspondingly short from hock to foot. The leverage in this conformation is conducive to great speed, and considerably reduces the strain on loins.

THE ART OF BEAGLING

Cow-hocks are unsightly, but the animal that is apparently thus malformed when standing still will often be quite straight when in motion. The question of the straight or bent hock is one on which the highest authorities disagree and the novice would do well not to bother about their formation, but allow it to be settled by the action of the hound when going at full speed.

My own personal preference in the general shape of a beagle is an animal on short legs, deep in the girth, and with nicely swelling ribs. A pack of beagles under 14 inches has, as a rule, to stand a much severer test of endurance than foxhounds. If blessed with good scenting powers beagles may be running continuously for four or five hours through changing hares, and unless built on sturdy lines will be worn out before the end of the day.

In stating my preference for a beagle to be short on the leg I would say that I regard him as a hound to be followed on foot. Foxhounds and harriers are for those who ride and may therefore be longer on the leg, in comparison with the foothound. Otherwise there appears to be no reason why they should differ. All want to attain the conformation most suitable for speed and endurance. There may be some slight difference of opinion amongst judges as to what is the

A FOURTEEN INCH PACK

right conformation, but most of them agree that shoulders, backs and loins with good driving power in the hindquarters are the essential things to look for in a hound meant for hunting.

FEET

In speaking of straight legs no mention has been made of feet. For a good many years the round cat-foot has been held up to us as the ideal to be attained, and I hardly like to venture an opinion against that kind of foot being able to withstand hard wear. A cat can certainly climb trees and go fast for a hundred yards, but her feet could not stand a long distance at any pace. The foot of a hare enables her to go fast and to keep up the pace for a considerable time without any apparent ill-effects or lameness. The harefoot and the cat-foot are extremes, but I should hesitate to advise anyone to breed his hounds to attain the shape of the former. Which, then, is the foot best adapted to stand wear and tear?

I can only give you my personal opinion of the sorts that do not appeal to me, leaving you to decide for yourself. My greatest objection is to the thin foot, and then to the variety with wide spaces between the toes. These two are generally condemned by all competent judges, and we can, therefore, hardly go wrong by agreeing.

The bulbous, fleshy foot does often pass muster in the show ring when accompanied by a straight leg, but it is a type of foot I dislike, and believe it to be ill suited to stand hard work. After eliminating these three we are obliged to join issue with the verdict of most judges that the small, round foot with toes close together is correct.

The novice cannot do better than follow on those lines in his desire to breed perfection, and he must not allow himself to be led astray by my reflections on the possible advantage of " back at the knee " or an elongated foot.

A good spring of rib ensures room for heart and lungs to play their several parts without pressure from any food left in the stomach, but a hound that is exceptionally deep in the girth may be forgiven if he fails in spring of ribs. When it comes to a question of breeding the continued use of flat-sided sires would eventually lead to a race of weeds " herring gutted " and shallow.

Legs, feet and contour are things the man who wants to have his pack of the approved standard may have to consider, but, as has already been

THE HOUND

said, shoulders, backs and loins with the propelling power in hindquarters are essentials for a hound meant to hunt.

Shoulders are in my opinion the most important points in conformation, but as the best judges often fail to satisfy themselves as to whether a hound seen only on the flags has good, bad, or indifferent shoulders the novice had better trust to the only reliable test of seeing the animal move swiftly over rough ground.

In Mr. Clapham's very interesting book, *Foxes, Foxhounds and Foxhunting*, he goes very thoroughly into the question of shoulders. All who have given thought to the question will agree with him that the excellence of a shoulder depends on the slope of shoulder-blade or scapula. The upright is, of course, the worst form. Determining how well the slope is laid back and how far forward the joint is in relation to the forelegs, are the chief difficulties in deciding the question of shoulders. A loaded shoulder—heavy at the point—is not as a rule conducive to speed, but a hound thus apparently handicapped may have the compensating advantage of a well-laid back shoulder-blade.

After many years of experience I must confess that, except in glaring cases, my judgment on shoulders never gives me entire satisfaction. What we call " balance," which means the whole structure of the body, in perfect harmony, is liable to upset the well-considered decision of those who endeavour to differentiate between the good shoulder and the bad.

A long back is to be avoided, and, though a little length may be forgiven in bitches, the use of sires with long backs would tend in time to produce a sausage-like animal. A cursory glance may leave the impression of a long back, but a careful scrutiny will often discover that the point of a shoulder-blade is laid so far back, and hindquarters so far advanced, that what appeared a long back is in reality short. It will thus be seen that the attempt to form a just estimate of a hound's conformation bristles with contradiction and difficulties, so that those with the greatest experience are liable to make mistakes.

This book is meant chiefly for the novice and he would do well to base his decision on conformation by the supreme test of a hound's ability to move. At the same time he can ponder over these suggestions and with these, coupled with careful observation, may eventually be able to distinguish the hound best suited to its work in the hunting field.

THE HOUND

NOSE

Although courage, stamina and mobile strength are indispensable in a hound that has to go through a hard day's hunting, they in themselves are useless without tenderness of nose, and without that qualification would be little better than a greyhound. Nearly every variety of dog has retained from distant forebears some measure of a keen sense to detect a difference in smells, but with hounds it has been kept alive by generations of careful breeding and a devotion to hunting a line. In the days that are past breeders may have often neglected to improve the appearance of their hounds, but they never forgot to make hunting qualities their chief aim. The result is that we have inherited the strains of blood which had proved most reliable, but we are apt to forget that in those strains there may have been sometimes an individual not above reproach. Should the erring ancestor's faults reappear after many generations we are inclined to excuse his shortcomings on the strength of other staunch blood in his veins, particularly if he should happen to possess looks that please the eye.

THE ART OF BEAGLING

CHARACTER AND EXPRESSION

Because a hound has, according to all available records, no hint of an ancestor with a blotch on his character, it does not follow the descendant of to-day has not inherited some fault from an individual in the dim and distant past of which we know nothing. Though it may be a throwback for many generations, it is a dangerous policy to assume that the good blood in the pedigree will counteract the stain. To breed from such is to risk the reincarnation of a sin that was in process of gradual elimination.

No hound man of any repute would be likely to breed from an animal with any glaring fault in his work. However, it is not only the absence of faults we should look for, but the possession of exceptional virtues in those we intend to be the parents of future generations. Never to breed from anything that has not proved itself in the hunting field is a golden rule, but that is a subject which will be dealt with in a future chapter.

There is an old saying that horses and hounds will run in all shapes, which means that the speedy race-horse or the fastest hound is not always built on the lines we have believed to be correct. If these cases were looked into it would generally

THE HOUND

be found that, although when picked to pieces the animal failed to fill the eye, it possessed the redeeming feature of "balance." Balance is difficult to define and detect, but it is the most important conformation in either horse or hound, and without it what we might consider a perfect specimen is a failure.

The head and the expression may not have much to do with the ability of a hound to perform its duties or, as assistants, to win prizes, but that they do give some idea of inner qualities is a fact beyond dispute. Expression is undoubtedly an index to character, but the reading of it cannot be explained or the meaning thereof set down in the written word. For the benefit of beagle owners in the future it would be a good plan if every master set down a faithful character of each hound's hunting qualities, nose, tongue and stamina, not forgetting any tendency to vice. Such a history would be invaluable to breeders, as they would then have something to go on in selecting strains of blood, for there is no doubt that both virtues and vices do reappear after lying dormant a generation or two.

Occasionally I see a hound that, quite apart from show points, appeals very strongly to me, and the impression thus gained has never yet played me false, but it would be impossible to say what particular feature caught my fancy.

Hounds are as varied in character and expression as human beings. However much they may be alike in other respects, no two hounds ever have exactly the same expression.

This is not meant as advice to the beginner in the choice of his pack, but still he might do worse than study the features of each individual member, and if he is a real dog lover he will gain an insight into their characters.

PURCHASE, PRICES AND LUCK

The man who wants to start a pack of beagles would be wise not to rush in at once and buy anything that is offered before he knows something about them. My advice would be to spend a whole season in visiting every pack in England, and having a day's hunting with each, at the same time taking down notes of the hounds that do the best work. He would thus learn which was the best working blood and glean many wrinkles from the methods as well as the mistakes of various huntsmen. When he finally decides on the height he intends to keep he may be able to get from packs of a bigger size a few old, trusted hounds

THE HOUND

that are no longer able to run up, but would probably do another season with a smaller pack. It is fairly safe to assume that anything kept for six or seven seasons must have been a reliable hunter. These bigger hounds might spoil the look of the pack, but as previously stated it does not matter what they look like if they only run level; thus an old 15-inch hound would be about equal to younger ones of 14 inches.

The annual beagle sale at Leicester is an excellent opportunity for acquiring unentered hounds, and it gives a chance of comparing sizes. A buyer should, however, be wary of purchasing entered hounds, unless he can get a character for them from someone on whom he can rely, as no one is likely to sell except for some fault. The unentered are, however, usually drafted for size, and if bred by a pack that has a good reputation for work are pretty certain to hunt.

The unentered thus bought should be of the size at which the pack is intended to be kept, but young hounds in their first season cannot be expected to hunt with the steadiness of veterans, and the old ones recommended would be required to teach them. Hounds drafted because they have become too old and slow can generally be had for a small sum, or perhaps as a gift, but in

THE ART OF BEAGLING

the latter case the giver usually stipulates that old favourites should be "put down" and not sold, when they have served their purpose as tutors to the young.

In the purchase of hounds it is almost impossible to give any idea of price as it may vary from one guinea up to a hundred for each hound. A very good pack of about fifteen couples was sold a few years ago, on the death of the owner, for £500, but with a little luck, and taking a large proportion of unentered hounds, fifteen couples might be acquired for about £80. The unentered hounds sold at the Leicester sale in May are priced by buyers according to looks, and there are often some very well-bred ones to be bought at a low figure. These may turn out just as good hunters as those that have fetched a lot of money.

The element of luck is always a factor at any auction, both for the buyer and the seller. Perhaps no one present may want the size you are after, and the result is that you, being the only bidder, are able to buy the hounds you have selected at bottom prices.

The importance of having a pack to run level has already been stressed and in buying unentered hounds it should be the endeavour to get all of the same height. Even when the same height they

THE HOUND

may not run level, due to some excellence in conformation or the reverse, but endeavour to select them as even in size as possible. The unentered thus bought will in time be the mainstay of the pack, and therefore care must be exercised in buying. It will be understood that the man selling unentered hounds knows nothing of their hunting qualities, and you have to take them on trust, but it is advisable to inquire about the working character of the parents.

If you are quite a novice with beagles you would do well to get someone with experience to help you in purchase. Suppose your purse to be well filled by all means buy the good-looking as they are much easier to sell again, and their produce are more likely to be saleable, but if money is short buy those which men who are only after the best-looking refuse to look at ; ascertain, however, that they are bred right. If prices are not too high buy rather more hounds than you will ultimately want as there are certain to be some not altogether satisfactory.

Although you may purchase a hound for £2 or less, it is as well to remember that a 14-inch beagle will have cost the breeder at least that sum or more before he is twelve months old.

The strength of a pack is in its youth, and to keep

THE ART OF BEAGLING

up that strength a few should be entered every year. To accomplish this the best working bitches should be bred from, and at least four times as many whelps should be bred as are wanted to put on. Distemper may kill off many, and of those remaining alive probably only a small proportion will be the right height. This will be referred to again in a later chapter on breeding.

PETERBOROUGH

Those who have attended the Peterborough shows for the last thirty years will readily admit the great improvement in exhibits during that period, and if we could be sure hunting qualities had not been sacrificed to attain this perfection there would be no necessity to labour the point. I feel, however, that nose, tongue and other important qualities have not gone on improving in the same ratio as looks. If the highest standard of field qualities is to be maintained, there must be an aim to improve it, or otherwise it will gradually depreciate. In breeding, as in other things, there can be no marking time; no satisfied complacency that the highest point of excellence has been reached; it must either go forward or go back.

THE HOUND

COMPARISON

Peterborough is in itself a very pleasant function and is an occasion on which beagle men can meet to exchange views. With only a faint hope of winning a prize I always advise owners to take what they consider their best hounds just for the purpose of comparing them with others. The hound that appears a swan in his own kennels may seem a very moderate goose alongside the best from other packs. The winning of prizes ought to be a secondary consideration, and though the kennelman may be disappointed at not securing a ribbon for his coat, you can console him with a reminder of your pack's success in killing hares. By a careful study of other people's hounds there is much to be learnt at this show and the novice should go back with a store of useful knowledge acquired. Because, however, the hound shown does not find favour with the judges do not discard him on that account, particularly if he is first class in his work.

SHOWING HINTS

Very few masters keep a dog hound or show him if he has any glaring fault in his work, but the

THE ART OF BEAGLING

ultimate prize-winner may be only a moderate hunter and holds his place in the pack chiefly on account of looks with the absence of notable vice. The seal of fame that is stamped on the dog hound winning the champion cup at Peterborough is a very strong inducement to masters of ordinary looking packs to use him, but unless they have proof of undoubted ability to hunt they run a grave risk of incorporating undesirable qualities. Judges do their best and probably make few mistakes, but it is well-nigh impossible to form a correct estimate of a hound's shoulders within the circumscribed space of a show ring. Therefore, what is supposed to be the best-looking dog hound in the show may have a faulty conformation of shoulders in addition to other imperfections in the hunting field. It will be seen that selecting a sire at Peterborough without having the opportunity of ascertaining his ability to hunt is a hazardous proceeding.

However indifferent a hound may be in looks, if he is the best in the kennel it is advisable to show him; his lack of the essential points to please the judges cannot be helped, but both master and kennelman should see that he is shown in the best of condition.

Everything intended for exhibition should be

THE HOUND

dosed for worms a month previously, and dressed. Then, after the dressing has worn off they should be brushed daily and a little dry sulphur sprinkled in the hair. My own opinion is that hounds should be shown practically in the same condition as when they are ready to start hunting, and that it is impossible to judge them correctly when fat.

In order that hounds should be fit and full of muscle, they must have plenty of regular exercise, but if my advice is followed on keeping a pack fit during the summer it should be in good shape by July, the date of Peterborough.

When judging I always look with grave suspicion on a fat hound, imagining that the layer of fat conceals imperfections the owner desires to hide. Perfectly good shoulders may be lost to view by a covering of fat, but the owner of a hound shown in that condition must take the consequences if the judges consider them bad.

Young masters of hounds are sometimes a little shy of exhibiting at Peterborough, but here let me assure them they will have nothing to be ashamed of if their hounds are shown clean, with a gloss and shine on their coats that speaks for itself of kennel management. Personally, I think more credit is due to the master and kennelman

THE ART OF BEAGLING

for the condition in which hounds are shown than for the mere winning of prizes. In this matter there has been a great improvement at Peterborough. A few years ago hounds came into the ring dirty, with staring coats looking as if they had never been brushed, and frequently with signs of skin diseases on them. Here is something we can congratulate Peterborough on accomplishing ; the force of example making masters and kennelmen realise the disgrace of bringing before the judges dirty exhibits. It may also, incidentally, have induced them to pay more attention to such details in the kennel.

CHAPTER III

BROOD BITCHES, WHELPS AND YOUNG HOUNDS

Whelping—Litter Feeding—Exercising Space—Doctoring—Walking—
Marking and Recording—Walking Prizes and Entertainment.

THERE is never a slack time in hound kennels and there are duties to perform every day of the year, but the spring is perhaps the busiest period; whelps are arriving and young hounds bred the previous year are being returned from walk. I will refer to the latter afterwards, and in continuation of hints on mating will discuss the treatment of the bitches with their families.

WHELPING

A bitch goes sixty-three days and is usually punctual to the day, but occasionally exceeds that time, though it does not follow that anything is wrong if she is slightly overdue. A dose of castor oil or liquid paraffin forty-eight hours before the expected date helps matters. If the bitch is

THE ART OF BEAGLING

naturally a gross feeder she should not be allowed to overload her stomach during the last week.

Unless the kennelman is an expert, and has the necessary instruments, it is better to send for a veterinary surgeon when a bitch appears to be unable to give birth without assistance. When a bitch has been straining, off and on, for more than four hours, it can be taken for granted the pups are dead or one has been turned. If it is the latter an instrument may be required to get it away. Needless to say, carbolised oil and disinfectants should be freely used. Bitches that succumb under these operations generally die from blood poisoning. Unfortunately these things will happen, but we can do much to lessen their occurrence by seeing that bitches in whelp do not overstrain themselves.

Dead puppies or those that have been turned are nearly always caused by the bitch having made an exceptional effort to jump a wall or fence. Nature usually teaches the expectant mother what she may or may not do, but hounds sometimes forget that obstacles they can easily overcome in their ordinary condition are a severe strain when carrying half a dozen whelps.

Although I have no professional or scientific knowledge, and may therefore be quite wrong, my

BROOD BITCHES, WHELPS AND YOUNG HOUNDS

own idea is that injury and displacement of pups before they are born is nearly always caused by jumping. For which reason I always advocate that the bench, for bitches that have gone a month, should be raised only a few inches from the floor so that they can get on to it without any effort. In-whelp bitches are the better for plenty of gentle exercise up to the hour they are due, but should never have enough to tire them or to cause any strenuous exertion.

A few hours after whelping the bitch may be given a little warm milk, but the majority want very little food during the first day; after that they should have as much as they can eat.

LITTER FEEDING

It is impossible to lay down a rule as to the number of puppies a bitch can rear properly, but I have always found that five is generally sufficient for a small beagle. Much depends on the individual hound, as some appear to have milk for a dozen, whilst others have barely enough for two. It should not be forgotten that as these babies grow they require more milk and that the mother's supply tends to decrease rather than the opposite. This means that when there is a large litter all may do well for the first two weeks, but after that they will start to lose their puppy-fat and the result is that growth is stunted. With more than five in a litter it is advisable to get a foster mother, or as an alternative get them to lap after the first fortnight, and should they refuse feed with a spoon. For very young puppies I always use Spratt's "Puppilac" and find they prefer it to milk.

Whether the litter be large or small I strongly advise getting them to lap at three weeks old or even sooner if possible. This is a job that requires a good deal of patience and perseverance as the youngsters seem to object to taking nourishment except from their mother. The object of getting them to lap so early is to teach them before they lose flesh and hunger forces them to take anything to fill their little stomachs.

With half a dozen litters arriving at the same time it will take a boy all his time to feed and look after them. It is the sort of job an intelligent boy, fond of animals and trustworthy, could perform better than a man, but of course under the kennelman's supervision.

Whilst the puppies are being fed the bitch must be tied up or she will leave little for her children. Moreover, when the youngsters are being taught

BROOD BITCHES, WHELPS AND YOUNG HOUNDS

to drink the boy will probably have to hold each one to the dish separately.

The beds should be cleaned out daily and fresh straw or hay given with dry sulphur sprinkled over it. See that the boxes or whatever the pups are housed in do not rest on the floor and that there is an air space beneath, otherwise you will be laying up trouble for yourself with rickets and other ailments.

EXERCISING SPACE

In an establishment where it is intended to breed extensively, whether foxhounds or beagles, there should be land attached to the kennels, and, when feasible, a farm of about a hundred acres. This might entail some extra expense, but it would be well repaid in the health of the pack and the whelps before they are sent out to walk. Some of the land might be under the plough as the soil is sweetened when turned up occasionally and it gets very foul when hounds are continually on it. For the moment, however, we are not concerned about adults of the pack and are only considering the welfare of the puppies. The ideal method is to set aside a certain acreage of turf for the benefit of bitches with whelps, taking care that the pack is not allowed on that ground. When the puppies are about three weeks old they should be taken from where they first saw the light and placed in movable kennels in the field.

A certain space, a few square yards, may be enclosed with the kennel, the fence controlling the puppies from wandering but allowing the bitch to get out. These kennels should be moved on to fresh ground at least once a week and those who have not tried this method would not credit the difference clean ground makes to the growth and general health of the puppies. Every autumn when the kennels are no longer wanted they should be done over with a creosoted mixture and housed for the winter.

The size of the kennel must depend on the size of the hound. My plan was to have a wooden frame with platform in front, the kennel itself resting on the frame, so that the whole thing was quickly moved. I do not pretend to know, nor can I give any definite reason why the clean ground should be of such benefit to the puppies, but my own experience has conclusively proved it to be a fact.

Breeding can be carried on successfully without these aids, but they are a help and minimise the ailments puppies are subject to.

(*Upper*) A LITTLE AIR AND EXERCISE
(*Lower*) A FINE LITTER

BROOD BITCHES, WHELPS AND YOUNG HOUNDS

DOCTORING

When over three weeks old the puppies should have their dew-claws removed, after which operation I always dab a little Stockholm tar on the spot to stop bleeding. Between the age of six and seven weeks they should be dosed for worms, and if looking bad in their coats should have a second dose before going out to walk. Always puppies should be dressed before being sent out to walk with a mixture of lard, yellow sulphur and a little turpentine. The lard is first melted and the dressing applied hot. It is generally wise to shut the mother away from the whelps for an hour or two after they have been dressed or she will probably lick away the dressing before it has had any effect.

Besides being unfair to those who are kind enough to walk puppies, it is very unwise of the master or kennelman to send them out full of worms or swarming with parasites, as the latter are generally responsible for a mangy condition later on. Hounds that are returned from walk with bare patches and the skin red beneath a scanty covering of hair can nearly always be attributed to slackness on the kennelman's part when sending out the puppies. Unless you send them out in good condition you cannot expect to get them back healthy looking. The master is the responsible person and he should see to this matter himself. If hounds come back from walk with skin trouble he should realise that it is a reflection on his management. Occasionally the person walking the puppies also keeps a lot of mongrels in a not too clean state and then the kennelman is not to blame. It is best to avoid these walks when possible, or otherwise to send over and dress the puppies whilst they are at their temporary home.

WALKING

Without walks it is useless breeding, and it is up to the master to use his persuasive powers to get members of the hunt or others to take the puppies. The ideal walk is, of course, a farmhouse not too near a road, but the increasing numbers of poultry now kept has tended to make the farmer's wife reserve the scraps for the birds and there is not much left for the puppy. Whether it be a farmhouse or a mansion, the mistress of the establishment is generally the individual who will look after the puppy and therefore should be the one approached.

The young hounds should come back to kennel

BROOD BITCHES, WHELPS AND YOUNG HOUNDS

early in March, as with young lambs about and small chickens they are liable to get into mischief. The first thing to do is to give them all a dose of worm medicine and repeat the dose in a week's time. Distemper is certain to come sooner or later and the after-effects of that disease are more likely to be fatal if the animal is full of worms. The dosing as advised to be given before the puppies were sent out may have been effectual at the time, but it will not prevent them from acquiring a fresh batch of these pests in the next six months.

I regret to confess ignorance of the different varieties of worms, but there are many and all are responsible for undermining a hound's constitution. However often you may dose, they always seem to come afresh, and like the poor, worms are always with us.

Breaking in to the restraint of a collar so that they can be exercised in couples is the ordeal the young hound must undergo after being dosed. Couples are very necessary to instil discipline into the youngsters who up to then have known no law and have roamed about at will.

Although it may save trouble later I rather hesitate to advise that walkers should be asked to put a collar and lead on their puppies when young lest they should be tied up, which is about the worst thing that could happen to them. The young hound that has never had a collar on until he is about a year old will naturally fight against it, and instead of coupling him to another, which will frequently cause a fight, it is better to tie him to a post for an hour or so. In a couple of days he is generally willing to go when coupled to an old hound and he is then ready to go out exercising regularly.

The sooner the young hounds are couple-broken and able to go out exercising the quicker they will adapt themselves to the new conditions and make friends with their companions. When possible, it is advisable to get the whole young entry in at once as then they are all " new boys " at the same time and start on the same level. Whereas the late arrival is apt to be bullied by those that have been in kennel two or three weeks.

The custom of keeping young hounds in kennel and not exercising them at once is in my opinion quite wrong. Up to the moment they are brought in they were probably free to range at will and the sudden confinement must affect their spirits, which means their health will suffer. They have to become accustomed to strange food and strange

BROOD BITCHES, WHELPS AND YOUNG HOUNDS

attendants. If, however, taken out for several hours daily, they will begin to enjoy life again and recover their normal appetites so that when the distemper scourge arrives they will be better able to withstand it.

When first taken out they should be coupled to old hounds, and whoever exercises them should have an assistant as you can never be quite sure what young hounds will do. They should be exercised until they show the first signs of distemper when they must be confined to kennel, but that dread disease will be discussed in a future chapter.

MARKING AND RECORDING

Whelps before they are sent out to walk must be marked. This is done by tattooing with Indian ink in the ear—an implement for that purpose can be procured with letters or numbers from Swaine & Adeney. Each litter should be marked the same and the numbers should not be used again for another ten years. One number will suffice for two litters, marking one on the right and one on the left ear. If numbers are used to indicate the litters it is as well to mark on the opposite ear one or two letters to signify the pack. Each foxhound pack has a registered letter or combination of letters and numbers which prevents confusion by two using the same. I have hopes that the system of registration will shortly be adopted by the beagle authorities. Puppies at walk, and later on when hunting, are liable to stray or get lost, so that when there is a registered mark the rightful owner is easily found. Anyone finding and keeping a hound thus marked would be liable to prosecution.

In order to get a mark that will remain for life it is necessary to rub ink in afterwards, as well as smearing the letters beforehand. The marking should not be done much before the puppies are seven weeks old in order to give the ears time to grow, but if there are several litters of about the same age that may get mixed up, it is advisable to clip a temporary mark with scissors.

The kennel book should be religiously kept, dates of service, whelping and ear marks written in at once with nothing left to memory. Failure to do this will soon land the breeding records of a pack in hopeless confusion.

Unless the master keeps these records himself he should make it his business to see that it is done, but the best method is for the kennelman to have his own book which he can refer to, and the master a more elaborate volume.

BROOD BITCHES, WHELPS AND YOUNG HOUNDS

These may seem small matters, but if records are not systematically kept breeding soon becomes a chaotic muddle.

Before the new master thinks of breeding he should ascertain how and where he can get his puppies out to walk. Beagle puppies are affectionate little things and when brought up with children are good playfellows. Those who have not undertaken to look after a puppy before may want a little persuasion, but it is the master's job to find walks before the puppies are ready to go out.

For the uninitiate it may be as well to explain the expression "walk." It means the care of a puppy for eight or nine months, or from the age of about two months until it is full grown.

Without walks it is a mere waste of time breeding. This is a matter the master must attend to himself, using all his persuasive powers to induce farmers and members of his hunt to take puppies.

WALKING PRIZES AND ENTERTAINMENT

If it is intended to breed any number, there should be a puppy show the following year with prizes for the best specimens. The prizes must depend to a certain extent on the hunt funds,

THE ART OF BEAGLING

or the generosity of the master, but they should be of sufficient value to make puppy walkers desire to win them. Although a hound's chance of winning will depend somewhat on the way he has been cared for, as a puppy, however well walked he cannot develop the necessary conformation to please the judges unless he is born with it. Some packs now give a prize for the hound sent back in the best condition, and many have adopted the plan of presenting a souvenir for every puppy returned. My custom is to give a small silver spoon, with the year and the hunt initials engraved, for every puppy brought into kennels. The spoons are each year of the same pattern, so that those who walk a couple or more are soon able to have a complete set. Teaspoons may not appeal to a rich member of the hunt, but they are articles the farmer's wife will always appreciate. It should not be forgotten that the care and welfare of a puppy nearly always depends on the lady of the household, so that she is the one we should try to consider and a silver spoon is only a slight return for her trouble.

Subsequent to the judging, it is customary to entertain puppy walkers and hunt subscribers to a meal of sorts. Foxhound packs usually give a luncheon, and a few years ago many beagle

BROOD BITCHES, WHELPS AND YOUNG HOUNDS

masters followed their example, but since the war things have become more expensive and the beagle puppy-show is now an afternoon affair with tea. Men may, perhaps, have preferred the formal affair with luncheon, but I think ladies are well satisfied with tea and it enables them to bring with them their youngsters, who would be a little out of place at a luncheon. It should be the aim of every master to encourage in the members of his hunt an interest in hounds, and the puppy-show does undoubtedly help in this direction.

CHAPTER IV

ON BREEDING

Picked Bitches—Qualities of the Sire—Balance—Quality and Looks—Babblers and Skirters—The Mute Hound—Period of Vitality—Inbreeding—Best Time for Birth—Dosing.

KEEPING hounds without breeding is like living on capital, and must soon come to an end. The strength of a pack lies in its young hounds and though some may carry on much longer, the majority of hounds begin to go down-hill after five seasons. There is, of course, the possibility of replenishing a pack by buying young drafts sold on account of size, but it is not always satisfactory, and by failing to breed from individuals that have proved their merit in the field, good material is thrown away and valuable blood strains lost to the hound world.

PICKED BITCHES

Every establishment that is not transitory and intends to exist for more than a season or two

ON BREEDING

should breed a certain number every year. Only those bitches should be bred from that have proved their value in the field. If the sires in the kennel are not of exceptional merit it is wisest to go to other packs and there select hounds that are noted for their working qualities. Avoid the first, second, or even third season stallion hound and look out for an older one. Constitution and stamina are essentials in the make-up of a hound, points which cannot be ascertained until after several seasons' hard work. A hound will sometimes be brilliant in his first season and worthless afterwards.

Although I consider the female asserts a greater influence than the male in those hidden qualities such as nose and drive, the sire must also contribute some of the virtues and vices he has inherited from his ancestors. Let us therefore consider the sire first and trust to him to improve looks rather than the dam. When it is possible to find a stallion hound that is good in his work, and his forebears for several generations in the direct male line have unblemished reputations, that is the animal to use. Some hounds seem to have the powers of transmitting their virtues in the direct male line, whilst with others it becomes swamped in the prevailing qualities of the dam.

THE ART OF BEAGLING

QUALITIES OF THE SIRE

If a sire is to stamp his image and personality he must have a strong head with a well-defined masculine character. The bitch - headed ones seldom prove successful and litters by them will all vary in type.

In the breeding of all animals, in order to get the best results, it is a fairly safe rule to remember that the sire should have substance and the dam quality. The continued use of light-boned sires would eventually result in a generation of weeds, so that a certain amount of bone is necessary, but not that excessive quantity which tends to make the animal clumsy. It has been said that bone carries the hound, which may be true, but it is also equally correct that the hound carries the bone and when that is out of proportion to the body it becomes a heavy burden.

After having ascertained a prospective sire's hunting qualities, the most important point in conformation is shoulders, and they are very difficult to gauge with the eye. Probably the only safe method of finding out whether they are good, bad or only indifferent, is to watch the hound in fast movement over rough ground and, if possible, down-hill. A smooth, effortless motion

ON BREEDING

usually indicates good shoulders, but even this is not always an infallible test. A hound with only moderate shoulders may appear to move freely and well for a short distance, whilst a lazy one—lazy when not hunting—with the best of shoulders will seem to potter in his stride. The only really reliable proof of shoulder conformation is the ability to go fast for a considerable distance without tiring and come out sound the following day.

This opportunity, however, does not often occur in forming an opinion of an individual hound belonging to another pack and we therefore have to depend on our reading of the exhibition he gives. The most expert judges will make mistakes about shoulders, and it is almost impossible to arrive at a correct decision when the animal is only shown on the flags.

BALANCE

Balance will often correct what appears to be imperfect shoulders, but then balance is rather difficult to define.

A well-turned neck is liable to deceive the eye and though good shoulders frequently accompany this type of neck, it is not always the case. A shoulder blade that slopes well into the back does appear to lengthen the forehand, but the very best shoulders will sometimes be found tacked to a short neck.

Conformation, as already stated, is usually transmitted by the male, which is my reason for dwelling on shoulders in selecting a sire.

Much harm has been done in hound breeding by men being tempted to breed from the mediocre on account of good looks. No one willingly breeds from a hound with any known fault, or is really deficient in hunting ability, but a particularly handsome specimen is allowed to reproduce its kind without ever having given proof of marked superiority in working qualities. Mr. Jorrocks very justly remarked, " 'andsome is as 'andsome does," to which we might add, " good looks do not catch hares." It may not seem wise to graft an ugly exterior on to future generations, but a hound with exceptional nose, drive and stamina that has run up for six or seven seasons is worth breeding from whatever his appearance.

QUALITY AND LOOKS

Improve the looks of your pack, but never sacrifice hunting qualities to that end. A hound

ON BREEDING

that shines above his fellows in tenderness of nose should be given the chance of transmitting that priceless virtue. Tongue is also of importance in a sire, and though you would naturally not use one that was mute, preference should be given to one with a good voice, and it is to be feared this has been neglected of late.

When in possession of an exceptionally good-looking hound, the owner is apt to follow the advice given to a woman on taking unto herself a husband, namely, " be to his virtues ever kind, and to his faults a little blind." This may be excellent advice for preserving domestic harmony, but it is fatal in hound breeding. No fault should be excused in either sire or dam, for although it might not reappear in the first generation it is pretty certain to crop up later on.

BABBLERS AND SKIRTERS

Babbling, that is, giving tongue when there is no line, is soon found out and the culprit should have short shrift, but skirting is a fault not always easy to detect, and an offender of this type may go on his wicked way some time before being discovered.

Both of these criminals do a great deal of harm,

THE ART OF BEAGLING

but the skirter is perhaps the worst as others of the pack may follow his example.

The real babbler and confirmed liar is soon found out by the other hounds, so that when they hear his voice they will utterly ignore him. In saying that a babbler was quickly recognised I perhaps made a mistake and a young huntsman should make quite sure before he condemns one as such. The scent where a hare has been travelling over night will sometimes last for many hours, and one hound with a very tender nose may be able to smell it when none of the others can own the line. It is therefore wise not to condemn on mere suspicion but wait until there is sufficient evidence to convict.

There are some people who consider hounds babblers that throw their tongues when first loosed from the kennels or enlarged on turf at the start; but with this I do not agree. It is merely joyousness of spirit and delight to think they are going to hunt. They are not pretending they have found a hare's scent, or attempting to tell lies.

The beagle is by nature a merry little fellow and it is a mistake to damp his enthusiasm. Skirting is a failing more hereditary than any other, but a hound that has run honestly for four or five seasons and taken a leading part, will sometimes develop

ON BREEDING

the habit when unable to keep his place with the pack. If a hound of intelligence, he realises his only chance is to make a short cut and he will go on in his evil habits, when he should at once be drafted to a slower pack. It is rather hazardous breeding from one of this sort, for though it may be the result of reasoning power it might be a hereditary taint from some distant ancestor, and as such likely to be handed on.

After suggesting that no excuse should be made for babblers or skirters, I have here set down a plea for their defence, but it is merely to advise the novice to exercise care in making his decisions.

MUTE HOUNDS

A mute hound will do more harm than a babbler, for though the latter will annoy you, his lying tongue will not deceive the pack, but the mute and jealous devil that goes off by himself will ruin many hunts. For this reason, and to preserve tongue, I am inclined to forgive a noisy hound if he is not an actual liar. Of course, the animal that lacks drive, ties on the line and is content to dwell on the scent without getting forward, should not be encouraged or bred from. Beagles should have as much drive as foxhounds and yet not flash on many yards beyond the line.

THE ART OF BEAGLING

All the above is meant as advice in selecting a sire, but is equally applicable to the dam. Although the male may constitute the chief share in transmitting conformation to the produce, he will also be responsible for an infusion of his own hunting qualities and those he has inherited. For this reason it is a great mistake to use a hound merely on his good looks. We should, or ought, to know the merits of our own bitches, but in going to another kennel for a sire it is not always easy to ascertain his true character. The hound that has run up for four or five seasons and is still in the pack is generally reliable, but have nothing to do with anything that does not hunt regularly. I have a theory, which may or may not be correct, that a hound of six or seven seasons will transmit the characteristics he has developed in life, whereas the younger animal will merely pass on those he has inherited.

PERIOD OF VITALITY

You may occasionally find it convenient to use a young sire of your own, but never use one from another pack. A beagle will retain vitality up to ten years and get puppies, but is it usually advisable to put these veterans to young bitches.

I fear we are all tempted occasionally to use our

ON BREEDING

stallion hounds too young, it does the hound no good and it is more or less breeding in the dark. A sire should have done at least two seasons and preferably three, with credit to himself, before he is asked to beget puppies.

Now let us consider the female, and, as already stated, in my opinion she it is that has the greater power of reproducing the hunting qualities she possesses. Breed only from your best working bitches those that have proved their worth in the field and have never done wrong. If you can find out that their dams in the direct female line for several generations have been noted for equally good characters, you have a sound basis on which to work. Sires may have been used in their breeding that were not without reproach but the strength of the female tap root will come out by judicious subsequent mating. Those who are fortunate enough to own representatives of celebrated female lines should cherish them and go on breeding from them until they can breed no more.

INBREEDING

When a bitch has shown exceptional ability in hunting it is a good plan to inbreed to her in order to stamp the progeny with that important virtue, but inbreeding should not be too close. With every instance of multiplying any given female line in a pedigree, care should be taken to see that the male line differs in every generation. The more inbreeding is resorted to the more important it is to trace the direct male line to a different source, and for twelve generations when possible. The direct line of both male and female exert a greater influence than intermediate lines. To achieve the best results, inbreed to the female line and vary it with the male.

The novice to whom this book is addressed may think some of the foregoing rather beyond him, and not worth thinking about, but the subject of breeding is an absorbing study and anyone keen on hounds should give it careful attention. Do not allow yourself to be led astray by the parrot cry that " breeding is a lottery." It may be if outward qualities are always expected to resemble sire and dam, without taking into account what each has inherited from its forbears. Breeding is a science of which we all have much to learn.

The dog fancier who wants to exaggerate some peculiarity of the breed to win favour at a show may achieve his end without much trouble, but the man breeding hounds for work in the field has a very different task before him. He has to think

ON BREEDING

of all the different virtues, such as nose, drive, stamina, constitution, courage and tongue, with the elimination of all the vices. By careful selection and without any reference to antecedents it would be possible to alter the outward form of most animals in comparatively few generations, but with hounds, appearance is only of secondary importance and what we require are these qualities hidden from the eye which have been cultured and stabilised by breeders in the past. In order to do this a very careful study of pedigree is necessary, but it should not be forgotten that an apparently faultless pedigree may sometimes contain a stain which might reappear, and a vice that had slumbered for many years be reincarnated to pass on to future generations. This means that because hounds are well bred, and bred from those good for work, they should not themselves be allowed to breed unless they have proved first-class characters in the hunting field. When it is possible to get hold of a hound of super excellence in work, either dog or bitch, breed from it freely, however much you may disapprove of its looks. Appearance may be forgiven in a bitch more easily than a dog, for reasons already mentioned.

Never allow yourself to be influenced by colour, as that is the last thing to be considered, and a

THE ART OF BEAGLING

craze that has lost to posterity some of our best blood.

If you are a novice at the game and have little experience you will have to take time before you decide which is your best hound. Do not imagine that when scent is good early in the day that the hound leading then and cutting out the work is therefore the best. At this period of the day, one in the middle of the pack may be your star performer, when with a failing scent and a sinking hare he will drive to the front to achieve a kill. It is also the latter end of a hard day that tests the stamina and courage, without which hounds are of little use whether foxhounds or beagles. The latter when small probably require more stamina than the former, as with a first-rate scent and too many hares they may be running continuously for four hours at top speed without stopping, a trial of endurance that foxhounds seldom have to encounter.

Then, having satisfied yourself with the hunting abilities of your bitches, first choice should be made of those with quality. Never breed from anything with really bad shoulders or you will be incorporating in your pack something that will take years to eradicate. Should the bitch be light of bone or be lacking elsewhere, choose a dog for

ON BREEDING

her mate that is extra good where she is found wanting. Do not, however, imagine that like begets like, as I have already said. You would do better to study pedigrees and, if possible, try to incorporate the lines of some bitch that has made a name for herself. In arranging a mating it is best to get the full extended pedigrees of both dog and bitch and to compare them together. Then if you can find some celebrated bitch appears in both, you will be increasing the chance of her good qualities coming out in the produce. If every huntsman kept an honest record of each hound's performance in the field, it would be of great assistance to future hound breeders, but unfortunately it is not done and therein lies the difficulty of making proper selections.

The subject of hound breeding is of such absorbing interest that I fear this chapter has become rather longer than was intended. There is so much to learn and the longer we live the more we realise that we are still a long way from knowing everything, either about hounds or hunting. I have just had a letter from an old friend, a master and breeder of foxhounds, in which he says, " Wish I could live. another hundred years and then I might know something." This is a man close on fifty who has made a success of breeding, and

THE ART OF BEAGLING

I quote his words to warn the very young not to think that a little experience on their part and a study of hunting works can make them fully wise. However, there is no reason why we should not try to acquire all the knowledge we can and glean information from the written experience of others.

BEST TIME FOR BIRTH

A huntsman would do well to mark off those bitches he intends to breed from early in November, as well as the sires they are intended to go to. Then when a bitch comes in use suddenly he will be able to refer to the list and not make a hurried decision at the last moment.

There is a difference of opinion as to the best time for whelps to be born, but although some people like to have them early in January I personally think March is quite soon enough. All young things grow best when the days are long and the sun shines. A puppy that is once stopped in its growth, from cold or other causes, will never develop properly. Unfortunately, we cannot arrange these matters at the time we would choose and therefore must allow the whelps to arrive when they will. The middle or end of November is quite early enough to put bitches to, but I hesitate

ON BREEDING

when to say it is too late as with a dry and mild autumn whelps will thrive apace. Repeating here what has already been said, do not be tempted to breed from any except the very best bitches, because the inferior come on at the time you prefer. Breed only from your bitches that are first-class in work, and breed from them every year until they die, and at any time. Ten years is about a bitch's limit to produce anything.

DOSING

The bitches that are intended for breeding should be dosed for worms early in November even if the whole pack have been dosed a few months previously. It is of the utmost importance to the pups' welfare that the mother should be free from worms. Whether the whelps acquire the worms' eggs *in utero* or take them in through the bitches' milk I am unable to say, but the result is the same.[1] The unthrifty pup with distended stomach and staring coat is suffering from worms.

When short of hounds huntsmen are often inclined to take out hunting bitches that are in whelp, and though it may not do much harm for

---

[1] It is believed that the spores or eggs of the worm are taken in by whelps from the bitch whilst suckling.

THE ART OF BEAGLING

the first three weeks a month should always be the limit. With old bitches that have to exert themselves to keep up with the pack it is perhaps wiser not to let them hunt after they are in whelp. They should, however, be exercised regularly and after about the sixth week they should be allowed to run loose if they do not go off hunting on their own, or the kennels are not near a main road. A grass run for hounds is an abomination to me and the only use for one is to give the in-whelp bitches a chance of taking gentle exercise.

CHAPTER V

KENNELS AND KENNEL MANAGEMENT

Ventilation—Brick v. Wood—Kennel Lameness and Floor Ventilation—Roof and Windows—Yard Space and Aspect—Drain-traps—Accommodation and Overcrowding—General Design and Details—Feeding—Change of Diet—Feeding Times—Appetites—Summer Exercise and Condition—Discipline—Medicine and Dipping.

THE success of a pack in the field is founded on its treatment in kennel. Kennels to house beagles may be in old buildings converted to the purpose, but when the purse allows and the pack is meant to be a permanent institution, it is better to build.

VENTILATION

Whether the building be new or old it should be both warm and dry, thoroughly ventilated, but without draughts. When hounds come home after hunting they want to have a dry bed and be warm. The ventilating question should be studied from both its winter and its summer point of view, provision being made for admitting more air in summer. Brick is to be preferred to wood and the less of the latter material there is in a kennel the better.

If the master starting a new pack and proposing to build kennels had sufficient spare time, with the necessary capital, he would do well to acquire a small farm of a hundred acres or less. Such an arrangement is ideal and has numerous advantages. Hounds could be walked out without going over the same ground every day and without trespassing on other people's land. Owing to the increase in motor traffic the risk of walking out on roads is every day becoming more acute. The farm would supply ample space for bitches with their whelps to be moved frequently on to fresh ground. A few sheep could be kept so that the young hounds could be given an opportunity of learning they must not chase mutton, whereas a farmer, however friendly to the hunt, might object to his flock being used to teach them a lesson. The master by becoming an agriculturalist himself would be better able to understand and sympathise with those over whose land he hunted.

On hired land most people object to putting up a building they cannot remove and which reverts to the landlord on the termination of the lease. Wooden kennels are then necessary, but I would strongly advise that all the wood is creosoted, not just painted on the outside but forced in by heat. This prevents insects and disease-germs from finding a temporary home.

BRICK OR WOOD

Whether the kennel be of brick or wood I suggest that panels of enamelled sheet iron should be fixed from the floor and surround the walls of lodging rooms—a sort of dado about 3 ft. 6 ins. high. Enamelled white, this looks well, is easily washed and does not harbour vermin. There is always a certain amount of grease from hounds' coats not easy to remove from wood, but with the aid of a little soda is quickly cleaned from the surface of enamelled paint.

The lodging rooms are the most important features of a kennel and great care should be exercised in their erection. Should the superstructure be only of timber the flooring must be concrete with all drains, of course, outside.

KENNEL LAMENESS AND FLOOR VENTILATION

For many years I have advocated a system of having a continuous current of air beneath the lodging room floors, so that all moisture from washing down and also from the earth has a

THE ART OF BEAGLING

chance of drying. This eliminates all danger of kennel lameness, a form of rheumatism which may incapacitate a whole pack. Although difficult to trace to its source, I feel quite sure this com-

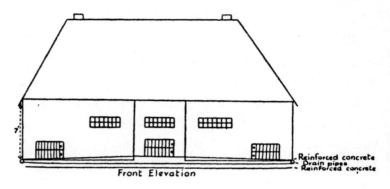

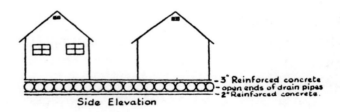

plaint is caused by the warmth of hounds drawing up moisture from the earth. The old remedy was to puddle clay beneath the floor, and as clay in that state is less pervious to moisture than any other material, it was fairly successful, but clay is not absolutely impervious and it does not guard against the damp sinking from above either of

KENNELS AND KENNEL MANAGEMENT

washing down or hounds' urine. My advice is to lay rows of agricultural 3-inch drain-pipes on cement, and cement above. The ends of pipes should, of course, be open outside the building and protected by wire netting from rats. By this means there is a continuous current of air flowing through and drying up all damp either from above or below. There are probably few kennels not thus treated of which the floors of lodging rooms are ever dry in winter.

To strengthen the flooring it is as well to reinforce the concrete above the tiles with steel wire netting.

If it is intended to build the kennels of wood I imagine they would at least be on a brick foundation. When this is done arrangements must be made for the drain-pipes' outlets. If timber is used the pipes may go through to the outside, one or two layers of brick being laid on top to keep them firm. This would be cheaper than building in iron gratings. Builders and architects might doubt the strength of drain-pipes to support a heavy brick structure, but this, I believe, might be overcome by a reinforced concrete foundation.

Anyone, therefore, building kennels should take some trouble about airing the floors of lodging rooms for the important reason mentioned, and

THE ART OF BEAGLING

also to prevent fewer hounds being lost through the after-effects of distemper.

The pipe ends must, of course, be higher than the outside ground level and above any chance of surface water.

ROOF AND WINDOWS

The roof is also of great importance and it should be constructed of material to keep out the heat of summer and the cold of winter. For that reason I would ignore galvanised iron and without much experience of asbestos roofing it seems to me suitable for the purpose. Whatever is used it is always advisable to have a double roof with an air space between.

There must be ventilation, but it should be so arranged that no draught blows down on the hounds. Windows that can be opened in the daytime are an advantage, and if there are windows at the back as well as front, both can be opened when the pack is hunting or at exercise.

YARD-SPACES AND ASPECT

A grass yard where hounds are allowed to run loose all day is an abomination and encourages bad habits.

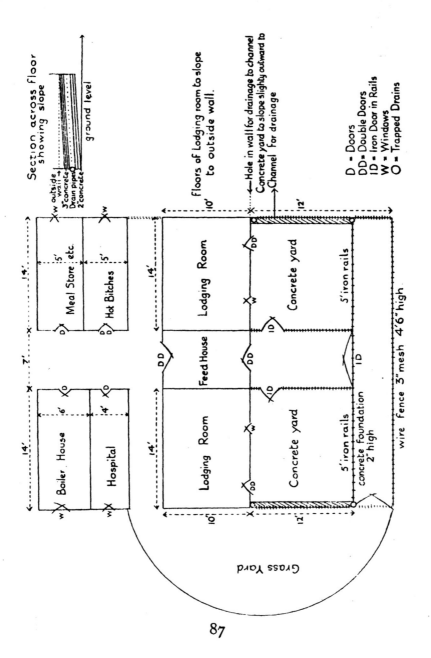

THE ART OF BEAGLING

An enclosed grass run is all very well if it is only used when the lodging rooms are being cleaned, and few beagle establishments keep sufficient staff to exercise as well as wash down at the same time. When only one kennelman is kept, walking out after feeding is an awkward business, and an enclosed field is then useful.

A south-east aspect is my ideal for kennels as they get the morning sun, and in the summer are shaded from the afternoon blaze. A concrete yard should be attached to each lodging room, in which hounds can run out in the daytime, but in very hot weather they are better shut up. I prefer concrete to slabs of that material because the joints are always liable to crack in time, allowing urine to filter through, which in a few years will saturate the soil beneath and set up a poisonous smell injurious to health.

DRAIN TRAPS

Both in yards and lodging rooms there should be a slight fall in the floors, just sufficient for the water to drain off. Drains would naturally be trapped, but it is advisable to have a system of double trapping with facilities for lifting the first grating and cleaning out the trap occasionally.

(*Upper*) READY FOR THE FRAY. A FOURTEEN INCH PACK IN THE KENNEL YARD
(*Lower*) TRANSPORT FROM KENNEL TO MEET BY LIGHT MOTOR CAR TRAILER.

KENNELS AND KENNEL MANAGEMENT

A certain amount of straw gets washed down and is always liable to stop a drain.

ACCOMMODATION AND OVERCROWDING

When financial considerations allow of a little extra expenditure it is as well to have two kennels for both dogs and bitches, so that they can be shifted daily from one to the other, which gives the lodging rooms a chance to dry after being washed down. The one yard would suffice for the two lodging rooms. The best arrangement is to have the feeding place in the centre with boiler house, etc., at the back. A gangway to the feeding house should divide dogs from bitches. If they are too close, bloody quarrels will arise and some morning you may find your best hound a mangled corpse.

GENERAL DESIGN AND DETAILS

All doors to lodging rooms and feed house should be in two halves, the lower half not higher than a smallish man's armpits.

It has already been advised that there should be a gangway between the dogs' and bitches' yards, although it means an extra length of railing, and it is also a good plan to have galvanized iron fixed to the base of the railings about 2 feet high. Some people prefer to have their yard enclosed by galvanized iron instead of railings. If close to a road hounds certainly do not get disturbed by every passing stranger, but if they can see out through open railings they become familiar with sights and sounds they are likely to encounter when hunting or at exercise.

The importance of having separate kennels for dogs and bitches has been emphasized already, but if the finances will admit of the extra expense it is a good plan to have a small kennel for hot bitches only, which should be so constructed that the most active bitch cannot get out, or a stray dog get in.

A wandering cur, such as a sheep dog or Airedale, might easily surmount a fence impossible for a 14-inch beagle. Therefore guard against danger from outside, but at night time hot bitches should always be shut in their lodging rooms to avoid risk.

When giving instructions to the builder on concreting the floor of lodging rooms he should be told that all corners should be rounded off. The same system should also be applied in concreting yards, as dirt, dust and filth collect in the corner, forming a right angle.

KENNELS AND KENNEL MANAGEMENT

This is only a rough outline of a kennel, but it will give a novice some idea. If going to the expense of building I should strongly advise making accommodation for double the number he intends to keep at first. Packs have a habit of increasing and hounds never do well when overcrowded.

FEEDING

The best food for hounds in hard work is sound horse flesh and oatmeal pudding, or in other words, porridge allowed to cool until it becomes a solid pudding. Unless, however, there is a proper boiler and the man attending knows his business, it is better to be satisfied with biscuits. In my opinion oatmeal insufficiently cooked is bad for hounds. There must be a separate boiler for flesh, in which, however, vegetables, cabbages and carrots (first minced) can be cooked. Nettles may be used instead of cabbage in spring and summer as they are an excellent blood purifier. When boiled down well with the flesh the results will be speedily seen in the improvement in hounds' coats.

Special boilers are made by certain firms for cooking oatmeal by steam, which prevents the risk of burning, and if finances will run to the expense it would be advisable to install one.

THE ART OF BEAGLING

The question of expense in initial outlay is frequently a serious one to those starting a pack of beagles and they must in consequence be satisfied with less complete methods. An ordinary iron boiler will do for boiling flesh. Biscuits though expensive are more convenient and save cooking oatmeal which will take up a good deal of the kennelman's time. Returned ship and other cheaper brands of biscuit containing no meat do well for the summer; but for the hunting season my personal preference is for Spratt's plain oatmeal biscuits, which with the addition of meat enable hounds to do a hard day's work, and return to kennels with their sterns up.

The biscuit broken up should be soaked at least twelve hours before use with the boiling soup and the cooked flesh mixed with it. Hounds should never have food hotter than just blood warm, as it is unnatural and injurious to their digestive powers. An ordinary farm cake-breaker is a useful implement for breaking biscuit, and a great saving of time and labour.

CHANGE OF DIET

During the summer it is a good plan to give hounds a variety of different foods, a change of

KENNELS AND KENNEL MANAGEMENT

diet being as beneficial to them as it is to human beings. Where it is possible to get offal from a fishmonger, heads, tails and the bones left after filleting, these may be substituted for flesh. Fish bones are more or less soluble and when boiled down make a valuable soup for soaking biscuit.

Where there are two boilers, rice is an excellent summer feed, but it requires very careful cooking and should be soaked twenty-four hours before starting to boil it. In several foxhound kennels where the question of feeding has received much attention it is the custom now to mix a certain amount of rice with the oatmeal, each, of course, boiled separately, and the mixture is used even in the hunting season. Never having tried it myself in the winter it would be hardly fair to give a definite opinion, but I cannot believe that rice contains the nutriment to support hounds in a hard day's work, that is possessed by either oat or wheat meal.

Food may be made moderately sloppy in the summer, but in the season should be thick. If hounds distend their stomachs with a lot of liquid it will not put muscle on their backs, and leave them weak and empty at the end of a long day. Our foxhound friends cannot be taught much in the matter of hound feeding, but I think some

THE ART OF BEAGLING

of them make a mistake in making the food too sloppy. The oatmeal pudding is broken up and after the addition of cooked meat—also broken up—the liquid soup is poured on. When this is given in excess the hounds may lap it up and by their distended stomachs show they have no room for more, but they have not filled themselves with nutritious food that will do them good. Hounds require a certain amount of liquid which they prefer in the form of water, but, in my opinion, unsupported, soup is not a natural food for dogs and when given in large quantities does more harm than good. One huntsman I know—a very excellent kennelman—used to thicken the food by the addition of bran which first of all had some boiling soup poured on, and then was allowed to swell. This was added to the food in the trough and well mixed up, the bran absorbing superfluous fluid and making the whole into a consistency that had to be eaten instead of lapped. We all know that much of the nutriment in wheat is close to the outer skin and therefore goes in the bran, but I am not quite sure if the skin itself contains any nourishing properties.

After a day's hunting hounds are sometimes too tired to take much solid food and on those occasions it may be given on the sloppy side. Hounds with courage and stamina may return to kennels after a very hard day showing no sign of exhaustion, but they will nevertheless feel the effects and the gross feeders should not be allowed too much.

The digestive system of a dog may not be quite the same as a man, but it stands to reason that neither one nor the other can properly digest a great quantity of food when tired. A further feed can be given early in the morning following a day's hunting.

Meat is the natural food of the dog and if fresh flesh can be procured I am a great advocate for giving it to hounds raw. By giving a leg or a shoulder at a time they can only tear small pieces and are unable to gorge themselves. Of course, it is necessary for the feeder to be with them ready to quell any attempts at a fight, but usually a word of warning to the quarrelsome is sufficient. It should be realised that allowing hounds to tear up and eat raw flesh is apt to make them fierce so that the feeder should not leave the kennel until they have settled down. Hounds fed on flesh are superior at the end of a hard day to those only given oatmeal and soup.

Keeping hounds in kennel is an artificial existence for them and the soft food they get is unnatural for a dog. When allowed to roam at

THE ART OF BEAGLING

will bones would be eaten and gnawed which are aids to digestion and at the same time keep the teeth in a healthy condition. It is obviously impossible to give bones in kennel, and as a substitute I recommend feeding once a week on dry biscuit. For small beagles, say under 14 inches, the biscuit should be broken to about the size of a walnut, which prevents them bolting it whole and obliges them to chew each bit. The kennelman may not approve of this innovation as hounds must naturally be allowed much longer to consume their food and he will have to remain with them until they have finished. When feeding on dry biscuits a supply of water should always be available.

FEEDING TIMES

The time of feeding is important on the day before hunting. Foxhounds that meet at eleven o'clock are usually fed the previous day about 8 a.m., but I consider for beagles twenty-four hours from the time of feeding to the time of meeting is sufficient. Beagles for their size have generally a more strenuous day than foxhounds, and through changing hares continuously may be running for four hours with practically no check. By the end of the day they will have used up all

KENNELS AND KENNEL MANAGEMENT

the resources derived from their last feed if given too soon, and will be drawing on their reserve of strength which means a loss of muscle and condition.

On other days, excepting those prior to hunting, the time of feeding can be left to the convenience of the kennelman. In very hot weather, however, I strongly advise the feeding hour to be put off to as near sundown as possible, bad feeders and young hounds will then eat heartily, which they would not in the heat of the day.

The kennelman naturally wants to get his work finished and go off, but if really interested in his charges it would be better to go off in the middle of the day and come back later. The evening is the natural time for the dog to feed.

APPETITES

Hounds vary considerably in their appetites, some are gross feeders and will gulp down the food in a few minutes. When these have eaten what is thought to be sufficient they must be turned away from the trough or they will take too much. Others are dainty in their feeding and should be allowed ample time at their meal of which they will never take too much. Perhaps it is not advisable to indulge these latter in the summer by giving them what is called a " second lap " and thereby encourage them in their habits, but in the hunting season they should be given all they want. These dainty feeders are a nuisance to a huntsman, but it does not follow that because they will not gorge themselves they have bad constitutions. If given time they will eat just as much as they require and can be trusted not to blow themselves out with too much. The general health and condition of a pack will depend very much on the attention bestowed on it by the feeder.

After feeding it is always well to walk hounds out for a short time, and when only one man is in attendance a wire enclosed field is required.

EXERCISE AND CONDITION

The end of the hunting season is the time to physic the pack for worms or other ailments and to have a clean bill of health to start hard exercise later on. Let me state here that in my opinion it is a very grave mistake to allow hounds to put on fat in the summer. With the cessation of hard work they will naturally fill out, but they must never lose their muscle and let it be replaced by

KENNELS AND KENNEL MANAGEMENT

fat, nor must they be given the chance of getting fat inside.

Fast exercise is, of course, unnecessary in the spring and early summer, but the pack should be taken out for long slow walks at least twice a week, and the longer it is out of kennel the better for its health. In this way the muscle gained the previous winter will be retained and when the time comes to begin fast work there will be no panting incapables lagging behind. The young hounds in couples will learn a little discipline whilst accompanying their elders and also build up muscle for the future. Discipline is very necessary and I am a great believer in the use of couples to instil it into the young. The couples can gradually be taken off a few at a time, as a lot of young hounds full of high spirits let loose at once may be difficult to control in the presence of lambs or other enticing objects to chase. Those of the young entry that have been walked in towns should be made familiar with country animals they are likely to meet out hunting, and those having spent their early life in farmyards, far from the madding crowd, should be introduced to busy thoroughfares.

The strength of the sun must determine the distance and pace of exercise in hot weather. When

THE ART OF BEAGLING

the sun is very strong it is a good plan to take the pack into a field where there is some shade and, if possible, a stream of running water, allowing it to play at liberty or dig up pig nuts at will. The kennelman or whoever is in charge can sit down and smoke his pipe, but, of course, he must have an assistant to control those with the desire to wander. This may not be very strenuous exercise, but hounds will be continually on the move, and it is much better for them, as I have already said, than being shut up in kennels.

The early hours of the morning before the sun has gained strength is usually considered the correct time for exercise and is the orthodox method in most foxhound kennels. My objection to this is that the men have a very natural desire to get back for breakfast and the result is that hounds are not out nearly long enough. If the early morning exercise is supplemented by long walks later on it is all very well, but by itself it is generally insufficient. Here let me repeat the advice—keep hounds out of kennel as long as possible, but don't turn them into a grass yard for more than a few minutes.

There is nothing better for hardening the pads than plenty of long, slow exercise on the roads when they are not too dusty and the sun not too hot. On commencing fast work ponies are useful assistants, but bicycles are perhaps to be preferred for road work, as with them it is easier to control speed which should be measured by the capacity of the slowest hound. The pace also must vary with the size of hounds and it is therefore impossible to give a rate of speed. For long bicycle exercise which should be twenty miles once or twice a week, it is safe to gauge the pace by the action of hounds. They should never be obliged to break out of a trot in order to keep up. At this pace they will be able to go on almost indefinitely without tiring, and if a good foundation has been laid in the early summer, pads will not get worn, and they will return to kennels as fresh as when they started.

When the season is approaching its commencement fast spins may be indulged in twice a week, and here again the pace must depend on the slowest hound, but it will be found if these spins begin about three weeks before the first day's hunting, the speed can be gradually increased. The importance of having the respiratory organs of a pack in good condition is not always sufficiently appreciated. When hounds check after a sharp burst, in nine times out of ten it is because they are blown and in that panting state unable to smell.

Furthermore, I would advise never letting hounds down in the off season, for though it may not be necessary to keep them up to concert pitch they should be continually at work.

DISCIPLINE

In respect of discipline there are some points which it would be advisable to add. Much can be taught in the kennel itself and one of the principal things is to make each hound answer to its name. This should be done with great care and without any harsh usage, but it is necessary in the first instance that the kennelman should have an assistant to put the hound called on to him. There is no necessity to raise the voice as hounds will hear a whisper, and shouting only cows them. Although it may take a little longer they should be drawn out this way to feed, and in the same way, when the kennelman considers the hound has had enough, he should call it back by name, when, if his order is not obeyed, the assistant should give the refractory one a tap with a switch. I advocate the use of switches in kennel as preferable to whips. If the same words are always used for the same purpose hounds quickly get to understand.

KENNELS AND KENNEL MANAGEMENT

Some kennelmen have been successful in teaching hounds to answer to their names without any assistant, but it is not an easy matter to call a hound that has not had a previous lesson if the same man has to hit him when he refuses to come. Of course, when once a pack has become accustomed to this procedure the calls will be answered like clockwork and an assistant is then unnecessary.

MEDICINE AND DIPPING

Hounds kept in kennels are, of course, living in a somewhat artificial state and require occasional doses of medicine, which to the dog running loose would be unnecessary. It is the custom in many kennels to give the pack a dose of sulphur, or salts, every alternate week, but I have come to the conclusion that it is better to dose such medicines on alternate fortnights. Epsom salts might be used at one time and Glauber the next ; the latter salts have more effect on the liver and should be used when there is a suspicion of the " yellows."

Some foxhound masters who have studied the subject carefully advocate the use of iodine, and there are firms who supply salts with that substance in them.

Cod liver oil can hardly be called a medicine

for it is more of a food, but it is as well to mention it here because it contains vitamines which are essential to the health of all dogs that are more or less confined. It will be found, when mixed twice a week with the food, to benefit the general health of a pack.

Pure cod liver oil is too expensive for general use in kennels, although for small puppies of from five to eight weeks a teaspoonful at a time, it is well worth the cost. Several masters both of foxhounds and beagles have recommended to me from their experience an advertised cod liver oil product called "Bicol." How much of the cod's liver this contains I am unable to say, and not yet having used it, cannot speak from experience, but I intend giving it a trial.

A good supply of cabbage or nettles and other green food might possibly supply the same vitamines. Care should be taken always to empty the copper used for boiling greens with the meat each time, unless it is kept continually on the boil. If the soup and meat are allowed to get cold, the greens which have been mixed with it ferment and in that state it is injurious to hounds.

If the kennel staff is of sufficient strength it is better that hounds should be brushed daily and sulphur occasionally sprinkled on. Dog parasites are numerous and a visitor from another kennel may introduce some which multiply with incredible rapidity.

It may be set down as a general rule that nearly all skin diseases owe their origin to parasites, and it is therefore of the utmost importance they should be killed.

As in human beings there are many forms of eczema and in most cases it is due to impurities in the blood, but at what stage it establishes a permanent hold on the skin I am unable to say.

The old custom in foxhound kennels to give the whole pack a dressing in the spring had much to recommend it, but the extra cleanliness and care of present-day methods has made it unnecessary.

With my small beagles I dip them three times a year in Jeyes' Fluid, but the springtime is the most important as then parasites of all kinds are breeding.

The homely flea is the easiest to kill, but the tick requires a greasy substance with a little turpentine to finish his existence.

The ear-mite which was unknown to me before the war has now become an unpleasant reality. Knowing very little of this parasite or even if it is visible to the naked eye, I hardly like to give my opinion, but believe it to be responsible for the outbreaks on head, ears, and over the eyes. In bad cases hounds may blind themselves by scratching at the irritation above the eyes. My idea, unsupported by professional authority, is that the ear-mite comes out and does this mischief. My remedy is to put powdered sulphur in the ear twice a week, but if spots and sores have appeared on the ears and head they should be dressed at the same time.

In all obstinate cases of skin disease I recommend the mixture :—

       25 parts black sulphur
       20 parts train oil
       20 parts Stockholm tar
       10 parts turpentine
       20 parts cocoa nut oil
       5 parts glycerine

The mixture stirred thoroughly and preferably applied warm should be well rubbed in by hand and in very bad cases a second dressing may be necessary.

The dipping process might be difficult with foxhounds, but should be comparatively easy with beagles. A bath capable of taking the whole body of the hound should be used. To accomplish the job expeditiously three assistants are required, one to hold the head, one the forelegs and the other the hind.

The hound is then immersed bodily in, the man holding the head taking care the mouth is kept out. The head man should also be supplied with a brush and when the hound is allowed to stand in the bath, head and behind ears should be well brushed with the dip.

The medicine chest might contain :—
    Flowers of sulphur
    Epsom salts
    Glauber salts
    Castor oil
    Cod liver oil
    Liquid paraffin
    Parrish's Food (as a tonic for sick hounds)
    2 gr. quinine tabloids.

There are probably many other equally efficacious vermifuges, but I have always found the pills supplied by F. Rayner, Haddington, N.B., give very satisfactory results, and have the advantage of acting as a tonic as well. They are only made to order and are consequently fresh.

The worm pills I get for whelps of seven or eight weeks are in gelatine tabloid form. What they contain has not been divulged to me, but they are exceptionally efficient in expelling the little thin round worm which infests young puppies, although apparently useless against tape worms.

As I have said, there are probably many other excellent vermifuges on the market, but I can only speak personally of those I use myself. Unless the kennelman has had considerable experience with hounds the novice master would do well to consult his local veterinary surgeon when in doubt.

In previous chapters the necessity for giving periodical doses of worm medicine has been advocated, but nothing has been stated about methods of administering. Most makers of vermifuges issue instructions as to the way they should be given and I can only mention my own practice. The most important point is that the hound should be fasted for at least twenty-four hours, and my preference is for thirty-six hours. The latter time is almost a necessity for heavy feeders and those inclined to be fat, but any that are on the light side may be fasted some hours less. After the medicine has been administered some sharp exercise should be given. On returning to kennels a little warm soup may be given, but not too much or the pills, powder or whatever the medicine is, will be brought up before it has taken effect. A dose of castor oil or salts the night

KENNELS AND KENNEL MANAGEMENT

previous is occasionally advisable with gross feeders. A dog will retain food for some time and unless the stomach is almost empty, medicine will have no effect on the worms.

The above instructions are meant for adults only. Whelps of from six to eight weeks should not be fasted more than twelve hours.

CHAPTER VI

THE KENNELMAN

Kennelman-cum-Whip—Disposition and Experience—Age—Housing—Duties.

KENNELMAN-CUM-WHIP

THIS is where it is very difficult to give advice because the man may be required for the dual purpose of whipping-in to the pack when hunting, and looking after it in kennel. If it is possible to get a really good man with experience in the kennel and one also able to run, so much the better. To be able to run sufficiently well to whip-in, a man must be moderately young and youth generally means a want of experience. The welfare of hounds in kennel is of more importance than turning them to the huntsman.

If the novice is unable to find someone with experience in beagle kennels, he would be well advised to get a man who had served his apprenticeship with foxhounds and was unable to retain his place through increasing weight. Perhaps not a man from a fashionable country as he

THE KENNELMAN

might expect someone to do the rough work for him.

The routine of most foxhound establishments could not be improved upon, and those having passed through it from boyhood upwards have very little to learn.

DISPOSITION AND EXPERIENCE

It is essential that a kennelman should be fond of hounds and of an equable temper, or with the power of controlling it, so that there will be no danger of his ill-treating animals which may annoy him at the moment. The kennelman must of necessity be left much to his own resources and in consequence care should be exercised in procuring references to character.

The huntsman whom he has been under would be able to give an opinion on the man's efficiency in his kennel duties, but it is the master to whom application should be made for personal character.

After ascertaining that the man has benefited by his experience to undertake the work of a kennel on his own shoulders, I should say sobriety, honesty and a love of hounds were the three chief things to be looked for in a kennelman's character.

Some beagles are highly sensitive and nervous

which would be increased by harsh methods and ill-treatment.

AGE

For a novice who is taking on hounds for the first time I should certainly try to find a man of mature age with a long experience in kennels as of necessity much must be left to him, and unless the master can be frequently at the kennels he has to depend on his kennelman. Sometimes a young man in the early twenties is available who has assisted his father since boyhood in some well-known beagle kennel and is competent to look after a pack as well as run after it. Should such a chance present itself the opportunity must not be missed.

Otherwise the novice had better cut out all idea of getting a good runner to whip-in. The majority of beagle establishments cannot run to the expense of two men, but when it is possible the best plan is to have an elderly man in charge of kennels and an active lad of seventeen or eighteen to follow hounds. If the right sort of boy can be found with an innate love of the chase, and being also what is known by many as " doggy," he will prove a great help both in kennel and in the field. Such a

THE KENNELMAN

lad if he gathers knowledge by observation and attention to his duties will in a few years be able to take a place as kennelman. The combination of an experienced man and an active lad seems to be the ideal arrangement.

Presumably the master will have " other fish to fry " besides the beagles and it may be either business or pleasure, but this means he will often be absent and he must have implicit trust in his headman. References may assist in gauging a man's trustworthiness, but these cannot always be relied on as no one when asked for a character likes to mention little failings. Before engaging anyone it is best to have a personal interview and judge from your insight if he is one you feel could be trusted. To advise a man in picking a kennelman is as difficult as advising him on the choice of a wife.

Wages will depend on whether a house or other things are found, but it is best to give a little extra and bar all perquisites. This is done in a great many foxhound kennels at the present day where formerly the huntsman had as his perquisite the sale of bones, grease, hides and so on. It is better these should be sold for the benefit of the establishment with perhaps a percentage on the sale to the kennelman. If there is no farm attached as has been suggested, the manure and straw can be sold or given to a local farmer.

Hound-droppings have a certain value, I believe, for some trade, but the small amount from beagles is not worth considering. Whatever may be done with soiled straw and droppings it should not be left lying near the kennels as it breeds flies.

HOUSING

Getting back to the subject of the kennelman it is best to give him a house as near as possible to the hounds, and if there is a lad to assist it might be possible to lodge him alongside the kennels. If you succeed in getting a really good kennelman and want to keep him, it will be advisable to find him a comfortable home, for though he might be willing to put up with any sort of a house, his wife would probably object.

Although there are many excellent and capable men who are liable on occasions to drink more than is good for them, it would be very unwise to engage one of them to take charge of a kennel.

Total abstention from alcoholic drinks is unnecessary, but anyone inclined to pass the limits of moderation should be avoided.

THE KENNELMAN

DUTIES

Any man of experience is familiar with kennel routine and knows what to do.

The first thing in the morning hounds should be turned off their benches and allowed in the grass yard whilst the kennel is being cleaned. I am not quite sure if it is wise to turn hounds out if it is a wet morning and more particularly if it is cold, but getting them out of the lodging room the first thing in the morning is an aid to teaching them clean habits.

The " walk out " in the morning and the same procedure after feeding are the regular duties of the kennelman and must be observed without fail.

The master should impress on the kennelman he engages his wish for super-cleanliness in everything, lodging rooms, benches and all feeding utensils.

CHAPTER VII

DISEASES

Distemper and Treatment—Jaundice—Chorea—Hysteria, Possible Causes and Treatment.

DISTEMPER

UP to about two years ago the annual visitation of distemper was expected as the usual thing in every hound kennel and probably carried off about fifty per cent. of puppies bred, but now that the *Field* Research has discovered the bacillus, and the way to counteract it by inoculation, we have the opportunity of insuring our youngsters against the complaint. Beagle masters are not usually monied men, and as inoculation is still rather expensive they may not all be able to have their puppies treated.

For this reason it will be well to speak fully about distemper.

Although letters have appeared in the papers of cases where the inoculation has not been successful, some failures were bound to be expected when the virus was first manufactured on a

DISEASES

large scale, but it is certain to win through in the end.

Although my means have not yet allowed me to make use of the discovery, I have had good proof that distemper is instilled into the system with the substance to neutralise its harmful effects.

Two of my best walks are in different foxhunting countries and at both places foxhound puppies are walked. Unfortunately my puppies went out before the foxhounds, the latter arriving a week or two later and both having just been inoculated. The result was that my puppies at both places were given the distemper and died very quickly, showing the germ supplied must have been exceptionally virulent.

Although rather afraid to introduce distemper in the kennel, I am, personally, quite pleased when all the youngsters have passed through the ordeal. Unless they do have the complaint when young, they are always liable to contract it late in life, and possibly in the middle of the hunting season. Hounds very seldom get distemper a second time, and if they do hardly ever die from the effects.

The two most important points to bear in mind are, firstly, to have your young hounds in good condition before the disease attacks them; and,

THE ART OF BEAGLING

secondly, when it does come, to destroy the germs by continual disinfecting.

By " good condition," I do not mean loaded with fat, but a state closely approaching that desired when hunting commences. A puppy cannot be too fat up to ten weeks old, but after that age, healthy muscle should gradually displace the fat.

Dosing the young hounds for worms directly they come in from walk is recommended, and as no vermifuge is any use unless the animal is fasted a day or two after they are back in kennel is the best time, because they usually go on hunger strike to protest against strange food and surroundings.

A second dose is advisable in a week or ten days, which should effect a complete clearance.

Then, when couple broken, they should be taken out regularly every day for three hours' walking exercise, not turned out into a foul and tainted grass-yard to exercise themselves, but taken some distance from the kennels where they can get fresh air and scenes. In this way young hounds, instead of sulking and getting depressed, keep up their spirits and enjoy the new existence. I may be mistaken, but it seems to me that hounds frequently die from distemper through not having sufficient energy to fight for life.

DISEASES

Some masters might possibly object because of the expense, as they would probably have to employ additional labour, but the wages of a man and boy for a month would be well spent if it saved half the entry.

The young hounds should be carefully watched, and the moment one shows any symptoms, or only a cold, the whole lot should be pilled with quinine. For beagles I use two-grain tabloids. The dose can be repeated every other day if necessary. This will enable them to fight against the fever which will develop later on. I have also used Lintox with success, but this, like quinine and other remedies, is merely a tonic, and unless given in the very early stages, is of very little use.

If you wait to administer a tonic or any other medicine until the disease has taken a firm hold on the hound, your efforts will be of no avail. Directly one of the young entry shows signs of having the disease, give all the others a quinine tabloid at once.

The Distemper Research authorities will doubtless be able to tell us, when they have completed their investigations, how long the microbe remains, after it has entered the system, before fever develops. This is a point about which I am very uncertain, but it is quite possible hounds have the disease on them long before the average kennelman is aware of it, which is a reason for a careful daily scrutiny of each individual. A dose of castor oil in the early stages helps to clear the stomach and probably some of the poison from the system. A very old remedy, which is not often used nowadays, was to give a tablespoon of common salt. This had the effect of making the animal sick, and probably answered the same purpose as the castor oil, but not having given it a trial I am unable to give a definite opinion.

Another old custom was to smear the nose with Stockholm tar, but although it can in no sense be considered a cure, it is very useful in preventing the animal from reinfecting itself and also from taking in other microbes which a system impaired from distemper is liable to absorb. The microbes of pneumonia, typhoid, meningitis and other diseases are hungrily waiting to enter, and their only passage is through the nose, so that the reason for using tar is apparent.

Probably very few hounds actually die from distemper itself, and fatal cases are generally the result of other diseases, the most common being pneumonia. When a hound's lungs are affected a pneumonia jacket should be sewn on and remain until it has recovered. In these cases it is of the

DISEASES

greatest importance to keep warm and avoid draughts. Fresh air is beneficial, but a draught is fatal. It is not always easy to get one without the other, but it ought to be managed.

JAUNDICE

The yellows, or jaundice, is a frequent after-effect of distemper, and although it is the result of the liver being out of order from a disordered stomach, a draught is usually responsible for bringing it to a head. Calomel is the remedy I always use for yellows, and when given in time will effect a cure.

CHOREA

Chorea, or St. Vitus' Dance, frequently follows distemper and is an affection of the nerves controlling certain muscles. There has never yet been an infallible cure for this complaint, but although very unsightly, it does not appear to interfere with a hound's running powers, and in many cases the involuntary twitches grow gradually less marked in the course of time. There are people who think that the predisposition to chorea is hereditary, but that is not my opinion and I

THE ART OF BEAGLING

would not advise putting down a promising bitch of good blood lines however much she danced.

By the use of tonics in the early stages of distemper you may be able to arrest its further development, but when once the disease has got a firm hold you must make up your mind to give the patients unremitting care, attention and nursing. Only soft foods should be given and they should be easy of digestion, such as Benger's or other things of a like kind. Hounds with a temperature seldom want to eat, and I think they are better without any quantity, but they must be made to take a little to keep up their strength.

The stomach appears to be the region chiefly affected, but whether this is caused by the distemper germ or some other microbe following on I am not expert enough to say. We do know, however, the stomach becomes ulcerated, and for that reason I call it typhoid, which may perhaps be a mistake. However, the result is much the same, so that we must avoid giving any hard food. Fits with accompanying brain storms are usually the result of irritation from something the patient has eaten, and frequently terminate fatally.

When the lungs are affected the patient with a pneumonia jacket on should be isolated and kept extra warm. Pneumonia is, I think, responsible

DISEASES

for more deaths in distemper than any other of the numerous ailments, and a hound suffering from this complaint should be kept to itself as it is a very infectious germ.

Here again it is important to impress the kennelman with the necessity for disinfection. A vaporiser should be used to disinfect the bedding and all surroundings. A method I employ which will be found useful is to put some hot coals in an old bucket and pour on them neat Jeyes' Fluid, keeping the kennel practically closed and allowing the fumes to reach the patient, so that the germs are destroyed in the nose as well as those that have been expelled and are floating about.

I cannot do better than advise you to pay a visit to an up-to-date fever hospital and take careful note of all the precautions employed to prevent the spread of infection. You would gather useful hints that would assist you in arresting the disease on its first appearance and minimise the chances of fatal results. The doctors have learnt a good deal in the last fifty years, with beneficial results for the human race, but we who have to do with hounds have made little advance on the methods used in ancient days. Dogs and men may differ somewhat, but the means adopted to prevent the spread of infection could apply equally to both. If, therefore, you are really keen on saving your young hounds from the ravages of distemper scourge, consult your doctor.

There is a similarity to distemper in influenza, but whether it is the same sort of bug that causes it I cannot say. Both are alike in that fatal results are caused, not by the disease itself, but by the after-effects, or the bugs of other complaints which the fever has permitted to enter. Then it is also noticeable that both vary in form in different years.

Sometimes distemper manifests itself with a soreness and heat in the foot, much resembling " sweaty foot," but with the usual accompanying peculiar smell. Frequently there is a swelling of gums and lips.

The distemper cough will often remain long after all other symptoms of the disease have disappeared, but I have no idea why this should be.

Finally, let me repeat the advice to keep your kennels scrupulously clean and free from smells, not forgetting to use disinfectants liberally.

Although it would hardly be a wise thing to dip a hound that had actually developed distemper, I have no hesitation myself in dipping the whole lot that have been in contact and may have the germs in them at the time. It is rather a drastic

DISEASES

thing to do and I am not going to advise anyone to try it, because a good deal depends on the weather and other conditions. I use Jeyes' Fluid and the water should be about blood heat. To be done expeditiously three people are required, one to hold the hind legs, one the fore and the other the head. My idea is that disease germs are often carried in the coat and probably parasites may not be guiltless of carrying diseases, so that the dipping will stop any further infection.

How much the Distemper Research has discovered as to the origin of the disease and its ability to reappear regularly every spring I do not at present know, but we shall eventually get the result of their valuable labours.

For a mere layman, with no knowledge of medical or veterinary science, it may seem impertinent to advance an opinion, but after some years of practical experience and observation I have come to the conclusion that the distemper germ is reborn yearly in the soil. Possibly it may occupy some host whilst underground, that buries itself deeply in the winter and comes to the surface in the spring. The germ then emerges with a new life and is ready to attack the first dog it meets, when it breeds and multiplies rapidly ; but with every succeeding generation above ground it loses power until by the autumn it dies out altogether.

Against this theory is the fact that distemper does sometimes occur in the winter. We know very little about the disease, and theories as to its origin can be only conjecture, but in burning straw and dung from infected hounds we can at least destroy possible means of infection another year. Then with a clean out of kennels and a thorough disinfecting of every place a sick hound has occupied we have done our best.

HYSTERIA

The *Field* Research have earned the gratitude of hound men by giving them the means of combating distemper, but in hysteria we are faced with a much more serious complaint.

The disease is easy to cure when taken in time, a dose of medicine with a change of food and kennel being usually successful.

The veterinary profession have thus far been able to discover nothing definite about the disease and it may therefore seem presumptious of a mere layman with no scientific knowledge to state his opinions, but there is no harm in setting down now what experience and observation have taught me.

DISEASES

The disease is contagious, but by what means it is impossible to say, though my impression is that the coat is generally responsible for carrying. It is a fungus and not a microbe, which means it can live on indefinitely in a kennel which has not been properly fumigated and disinfected.

The cracks in woodwork or straw fibres will enable this fungus to exist and subsequently throw off spores which either settle on a hound's coat or are conveyed direct to the nostrils. Also it is possible these spores may be contained in dust that to the naked eye appears quite harmless.

From my experience I should say the period of incubation varies considerably after the animal has taken in the germ. That is to say, as far as can be judged by the time the first symptoms are noted. If, however, as I believe, the disease first attacks the stomach, it would depend very much on the state of that organ, healthy or otherwise, how long it could resist the fungus. The irritation thus set up in the stomach is apparently conveyed by the nerves to the brain and causes the disturbance which drives the dog temporarily mad.

Perhaps my supposition is wrong that the stomach is first attacked and it may be the original trouble starts with the brain. We may take it that practically all diseases from which dogs suffer are introduced to the system by the nose channel.

The established fact that hounds fed on biscuit or other farinaceous foods, when given meat only, recover at once from an attack, is a pointer in favour of my fungus theory. It seems only reasonable to surmise that a fungus being a vegetable should be able to breed and multiply amidst biscuit or meal, whereas it would be unlikely to flourish on meat. A microbe being animal would naturally find a meat diet favourable.

In further support of my theory that hysteria is not caused by a microbe is the fact that the disease may be dormant for months, which unless occupying a living host would be impossible. A fungus could go on living happily in wood or straw for years unless destroyed by strong disinfectants or fire.

These observations have been gathered from my own practical experience of the disease and it would be best to give details of the circumstances.

Here then is a brief history of the disease in my kennel.

The purchase of an unentered hound in 1925, only recently returned from walk, introduced the complaint, but not having ever seen anything of

DISEASES

the kind before I imagined it a temporary stomach ailment and did not isolate.

This first case appeared early in June and practically the whole pack was affected by the middle of July. Change of food and dosing with Glauber salts were tried without permanent results, though the latter gave temporary relief. By the end of August I had come to the conclusion that it was a contagious disease. It has been my custom to take the whole pack in September to the seaside for a month and with the determination not to take the contagion with me, I dipped the whole pack in a bath of Jeyes' Fluid the afternoon before starting, leaving instructions that the kennels were to be thoroughly cleaned and disinfected in my absence. Although eight or ten couples had fits the day previously, there was not one case after the pack had reached its temporary quarters, and they returned home without any sign of hysteria. All went well then until the following year. When, however, saying the kennels were cleaned and disinfected I omitted to mention an outhouse which it was impossible to disinfect properly. In this outhouse a bitch with whelps had been placed in 1925. This bitch developed hysteria. Without thinking, this house was used again for a bitch in 1926, and she also in a few days contracted the disease. So my trouble began again, but by frequent dipping it was possible to limit the outbreak. From that time till 1930 hysteria would reappear occasionally without any apparent reason. Several had attacks in the late summer of that year and were a constant source of worry, and then again on going to the sea there was a clean bill of health.

The pack returned during the first week in October in excellent health and condition, two days later were out hunting, killed a hare and never showed the slightest sign of hysteria. It was eight or ten days before hounds hunted again and then several had fits. This to my mind was proof positive that the disease was in the kennel and with the assistance of the local sanitary inspector I thoroughly fumigated them. Before this was done, however, I suspected that the fungus might have a home in the straw lining the roof beneath the tiles, and which had been there many years. This was ripped off and burnt, but in doing so clouds of dust came down which probably settled in cracks and crevices which it was impossible to clear away entirely. That dust I am firmly convinced contained the spores of the fungus and several fresh cases occurred after the straw had been removed. The subsequent fumiga-

DISEASES

tion followed by periodical spraying of disinfectant with a Four-oaks sprayer which reached every crack in roofs and walls, in addition to again dipping the whole pack, has resulted in a permanent cure.

The excuse for giving this lengthy yarn of my own experience is that it may assist those who have the misfortune to get the disease to realise the importance of eradicating it from the kennel.

The idea that the disease was caused by a fungus and not a microbe was given me by a very clever American doctor, so that I cannot claim credit for its evolution from my own brain.

What has been puzzling those who have studied the matter is how the disease was introduced into this country. We know it was prevalent in America a year or two before it appeared over here, and if the fungus theory is correct it is easy to understand that either hay, wood or straw used for packing would bring it across without the necessity of a dog having the disease being a carrier.

The after results of hysteria appear to have more effect on young hounds than old, and those under twelve months that have had the disease are often slow to enter. Apparently a bad attack will leave an impression on the brain that may take a long time to disappear.

THE ART OF BEAGLING

It is perhaps venturing into realms beyond my knowledge, but I have heard the brain cells of human beings develop gradually with age. Is it not then possible the same process goes on in the canine race? If that is so it would be easy to understand when a young dog with the cells only imperfectly developed received the shock which hysteria gives, his brain might be permanently affected?

Whelps under three months only occasionally get the disease, but when they do it is better to destroy them at once as the chances of their being any good for hunting are small.

A proof of hysteria sometimes leaving an impression on the brain is that the animal, though apparently normal again, will have a fit when visiting a spot where he previously had an attack.

Until fully recovered, excitement of any kind will bring on a fit and hounds should not be hunted until all signs of the disease have disappeared. Contrary to the advice frequently given I consider hounds should have regular daily exercise, not sufficient to tire, but with fairly long spells in the open air. It is, however, advisable with hounds suffering from the disease to exercise in couples, for otherwise one may get an attack and run for miles.

DISEASES

From what has been written the reader will gather it is of the first importance to minimise any chance of reinfection by killing the source of the disease's origin. Dipping the whole pack and thoroughly disinfecting the kennels are the best methods to obtain that result.

I have one favourite hound, now eight years old, that lives in the house and never goes in the kennel, but hunts and goes exercising with the pack. She has never had the disease, which appears to me convincing proof that my theory is correct.

CHAPTER VIII

THE HARE

Pugnacity and Nerve—Tricks and Stamina—Wild and Semi-Tame—Preservation—Marital Relations—Leverets—Tricks.

WHEN hunted with hounds that are not too big the hare can take care of herself and frequently outwits her pursuers by aid of instinct inherited from forebears of a thousand years. If, however, her speed is nearly matched by the pack, she never gets the opportunity of putting in practice the many tricks of which she is capable. Such sport is too much like coursing to be called hunting.

My own idea is that the odds against the hare should be relatively the same as they are with foxhounds against the fox. A hare when first found ought to be able to get out of sight from hounds in a few seconds, and until she is beaten they should trust entirely to their noses in following her. It is only natural a huntsman should want to kill every hare found, both for the sake of hounds and his own satisfaction, but although

THE HARE

this result can be easier achieved by raising the height of the pack, much of the finer points of hunting are lost, and the hare is given no chance of employing her natural tactics. The fastest runner cannot hope to keep near 16-inch hounds when there is a good scent and consequently very little can be seen of what individual hounds are doing.

PUGNACITY AND NERVE

"Timorous hare" is mere poet's licence, although there seems a general idea she is a very timid animal, but the truth is she is both pugnacious and bold. What is considered timidity is in reality a very high strung nervous system attuned to the brain by a powerful sense of smell and hearing. The jacks will fight each other with the utmost ferocity and it is not uncommon to find one that has been slain in battle. They will sit up and box with the forefeet, when little damage is done, but they get busy with the powerful hindlegs, one blow struck home is sufficient to cause a mortal wound.

I remember a few years ago, about the first week in March and our last day of the season, we had been running a hare for close on two hours and

THE ART OF BEAGLING

expecting every minute to kill. Most of the run had been on low ground, but as a last resource the hare went up a hill and on the crest was attacked by another jack. The weary one, of course, made no fight, but endeavoured to get away, whilst the other kept butting it and as far as we could see, striking with the forefeet. The

FRESH

battle occurred only some three hundred yards from where hounds were running and this fresh hare must have heard them, which is pretty conclusive evidence that the cry of a pack does not inspire them with fear as some people seem to think.

From many years of experience and observation my impression is that a hare when first starting in front of hounds goes away light-heartedly and full of confidence in her ability to defeat her pursuers.

THE HARE

Inherited instinct enables her to distinguish quickly between being coursed by a cur or hunted by scent. Possessing herself a very keen sense of smell, she realises when hunted those places where scent is least likely to lie well and thus takes advantage of roads or makes use of odours from sheep to confuse her pursuers. For the same purpose she risks losing the distance gained in order to run her foil and double in her tracks, frequently making a big leap sideways and going off at a right angle to her previous course. Much of this is doubtless due to instinct, but some may be credited to reason, for a hare having escaped after once being hunted will adopt the same tactics, on a future occasion, that had saved her life previously. There are those who deny animals the power of reason, but if this is not reasoning—what is it ?

A hare perhaps is inclined to underestimate the danger from beagles and may think, as she can easily outdistance them when they are running her in view, that her superior speed will save her in the end. When feeling strong and fresh as she springs from her form, this is quite easy to understand, but the race is not always to the swift and though her pace is wonderful, the stamina of hounds wins the race.

THE ART OF BEAGLING

TRICKS AND STAMINA

I have often thought when watching a fresh hare get up in front of hounds that she purposely keeps only a short distance in front of them for three or four hundred yards in order to test their pace. People who have not observed this peculiarity will remark: " By Jove! did you notice that hare could not get away from hounds and they would have caught her if she had not reached the fence." When, as a matter of fact, she judges to a nicety the distance of the fence and knows exactly where to find a familiar smeuse which, with the power of looking behind in running, enables her to measure the pace necessary to attain safety.

Then again I have seen hares hotly pursued for some minutes, but not in view of hounds, stop on reaching a fence and sit up to listen. Of course, they know perfectly well it is not easy to see them in the shadow of a fence and it may be also they are a little uncertain of the smeuse's location, but having found it and discovered the way clear, they feel safe in waiting a few seconds to ascertain the enemies' rate of progress. The smeuses adjacent to a hare's form are, of course, well known to her, and she has also a general knowledge of other

THE HARE

openings further afield, but these latter may have been changed by the hand of man and it would be risky to depend on them being available at a critical moment. An old hare that has been hunted on former occasions realises the importance of

FIRST ALARM

reserving her strength and does not tire herself unnecessarily by sprinting, whereas the young and inexperienced go away at top speed and are too exhausted to make a supreme effort later on.

The country and the food to be found there have considerable influence on a hare's condition. In an arable district where roots are plentiful, or

THE ART OF BEAGLING

market gardens where there is an abundance of green food to be had in the winter, hares are fat and easily tired. It is the superiority in fitness that is the determining factor in enabling hounds to achieve their triumph.

The hare living amidst arable fields, in addition to finding plenty to eat without roaming afar, is seldom disturbed from her form during the day and consequently gets very little exercise.

A grass country may be an advantage to hounds in the matter of scent, but hares of those regions are very different to their plough land sisters. Sheep and cattle are in the fields the whole winter and have to be attended to night and day by the shepherd with his dog. The latter is usually a speedy animal and a hare must exert herself to get away from him. One that is at all weak is likely to provide the shepherd with a dinner, so that it is really a survival of the fittest. A grass-land hare may be disturbed from her form any time in the day, and, when put up, must run for her life. The nightly ramblings in search of food keep her in good condition, and she is thus able to defeat her would-be captors, unless having the misfortune to come within range of a gun. A greyhound has little chance of catching a really wild grass-fed hare unless it happens to be an

THE HARE

exceptionally big field, but the lurcher with power of scent as well as sight, in addition to speed, is a serious menace. The travelling tinker or wandering gipsy frequently owns this class of dog and they doubtless snap up many hares, but rich men who should know better are sometimes guilty of keeping lurchers, and take them out when not following foxhounds.

WILD AND SEMI-TAME

I have little experience and no sympathy for the semi-tame hare that lives an undisturbed existence under the watchful eye of a keeper until the day she is driven forward to a gun. Good sportsmen and men with the reputation of shooting straight, take little pleasure in the killing of a hare, and frequently repeating the operation becomes wholesale butchery. However, where hares are preserved it is necessary to reduce their numbers, as they do a great deal of damage to the farmers' crops and it is said ten hares eat as much as a sheep. They have a habit of taking one bite out of a turnip and passing on to serve many others in the same way, but where fresh greens are grown for the market they cause much annoyance and loss by eating out the hearts of young plants. The damage thus done by an odd hare or two is not noticeable and it is only when too numerous that the loss becomes serious.

The hare is by nature a very shy and wild animal, but when preserved and protected against the enemies which for many generations have sought her life, she changes all the habits taught by inherited instinct and loses her fear of man. On strictly preserved estates hares may be seen by people on a road running about the fields as unconcerned as sheep, and careless of being in full view.

On such ground it would be hopeless to hunt beagles as they would be changing every minute, although I imagine if hounds were able to stick to one of these tame animals they would very soon account for it.

The preservation of hares in specially favourable quarters is, however, an advantage to beagle men as they are able to restock parts of their countries in which they are scarce. When these hares are put down on strange land they should be treated well, fed and not disturbed until they have settled down—of course, not hunted for six months. In time they will get out of their habit of showing themselves unashamed to anyone who cares to look, and get back the cunning of their ancestors.

THE HARE

PRESERVATION

If it is desired to stock a wide area of country perhaps the best time to turn out is February, as then they will breed and are sure to stop. Hares

LISTENING

when turned down at that time of the year in an open country and where there is no covert, may wander some distance from the spot where they were loosed. If it is wanted to improve the stock of the whole district this does not matter, but when it is required to have hares in one particular locality, it is the best plan to get half-grown leverets and turn them down during the summer months in long grass or better still, in a field of growing corn if there happens to be one about the centre of the location.

They will stay there then until the corn is cut and can be considered fixed residents of the district. It would be unwise to hunt them often at the beginning of the season and not for some time after the corn is cut. Young hares that have lived in standing corn and probably only ventured for a short distance outside to feed, are rather bewildered when their ample covert is transformed to bare stubble. They must be given time to accustom themselves to altered conditions and find new hiding places. By the middle of the season they will look on the place as home and will be found when wanted. Unless the person who is turning out the hares owns the cornfield he had better come to terms with the farmer and arrange to be there at reaping time, an occasion on which no dogs should be present.

If you can get the farmer to go round the field three or four times the day before he finishes, the hares will in all probability move away at night and thus obviate the shouting from the labourers which usually greets their appearance.

THE HARE

A shilling apiece to the men working is money well spent.

The man who wants to have hares should first of all get rid of his rabbits, dig out and kill all he can. Hares and rabbits are found together sometimes, but the former very much dislike the latter and will wander away to districts where they are scarce.

The rabbit is a destructive little beast and in addition to eating everything, trees, shrubs and hedges, poisons the land over which he wanders. I regret to say they appear to be on the increase, and farmers will soon find them as much a pest in England as they did in Australia.

MARITAL RELATIONS

My knowledge of the marital relations existing amongst hares is somewhat limited and though works on natural history would doubtless supply the information, I prefer to write only of facts gathered by personal observation. The jack is certainly not faithful to one spouse and I believe the number of his wives depends on his ability as a fighter. Where hares are numerous and does in excess of jacks, there is generally peace, but when jacks outnumber the does, there are sure to be many bloody battles and the fur will fly. Perhaps the hare has been given here a character he does not altogether deserve, as I believe for the courtship and subsequent short honeymoon, he remains a more or less faithful husband, after which he wanders off in search of fresh conquests. Where they are thinly scattered, jacks will go for many miles in search of wives and it is at this period they afford the hunter his best runs.

How many young a hare has been known to give birth to at once is uncertain, but in my experience never more than five. In my country the average would be a shade over two, but is probably higher on more favourable soils. The difficulty of ascertaining the exact number is that the mother does not drop them all in one nest, but distributes them in various places, sometimes many yards apart, and is expert in her methods of hiding them.

LEVERETS

The little leveret comes into the world fully clothed with fur and well able at once to use its legs, which however it does not do except as a last resource, but has a marvellous capacity for taking advantage of a tuft of grass or uneven ground, where it is almost invisible. Were it not

THE HARE

for this instinct which nature has provided they would be at the mercy of carrion crows and magpies. The usual observer is apt to think the mother very careless in looking after her family, because she drops them about in what appears to him a haphazard manner, but she is really a devoted parent and her methods of leaving them in different spots is to ensure their safety. Two or three together would be easily seen, but it takes a very sharp eye to discover one. Then she never stops with them longer than to give them milk and will lie up until next feeding time a quarter of a mile distant, for to remain close would only be to increase the risk of being found. When disturbed the mother of a family immediately makes off in the opposite direction to that in which her youngsters lie hid, but she will circle round and be back again in the face of danger to tend to their wants at feeding time.

Leverets may be expected by the first week in March and often much earlier, depending on the weather.

The early youngsters have a hard time to escape their natural enemies as there is no vegetation to hide them and not many survive.

The hare is capable of adapting herself to circumstances which would appear foreign to her nature. There was a certain sector in France that had been so ploughed up by shells that there hardly seemed a square inch of unbroken ground. Over this sea of mud and holes our division went to a well-earned victory, and half an hour later I was discussing the attack in the dressing-station with the sergeant-major of my old battalion. " I

Last Effort

thought of you, sir, as we went over the top for the first thing I saw was a great big hare." How it was possible she could have lived for a month or more in that inferno is beyond understanding, and what she found to eat is equally difficult to realise.

TRICKS

How much inherited instinct or reason acquired by experience is responsible for the numerous dodges a hare employs to outwit her enemies is a

THE HARE

debatable question impossible to decide. Her many and various wiles are too numerous to catalogue here.

To push a fresh hare out of her form and take the other's place is a frequent trick of a hunted one when being pressed by hounds. The funny thing is that the fresh hare does not appear to make any complaint, but goes gaily on as a matter of course to lead the pack away from a tired friend. This seems an understood unselfish proceeding amongst hares and is a code that nature has instilled for the benefit of their species.

Providence or nature has probably given most other animals the instinct to help each other when pursued. On an occasion many years ago on an upland plateau in Western America I found an antelope with two youngsters, and being very anxious to capture one alive pursued, hoping to rope it. At the moment when the little thing was getting tired and it looked as if my efforts would be successful, the other would suddenly appear without my being able to see where the change had occurred. The result was that my pony was tired first and the young antelopes were left in peace.

A hare with the long hairs on her hind feet is very severely handicapped when they get clogged with mud. In my country where ploughed fields are few and far between, a hare when not closely pursued will stop to clean the mud from her feet in the grass. This I have frequently seen.

As it has already been stated a hare quickly knows when she is being hunted by scent, and

DEAD BEAT

having herself a very sensitive smelling organ will take every means to neutralize her trail.

The road is one of her favourite methods of making difficulties for hounds and she will also circle or run through a flock of sheep to attain the same object. A freshly manured field if handy will be taken advantage of when her enemies become pressing, and, though not having yet witnessed it myself, a hunted hare has been seen to roll in manure in order to baffle the pack. To double

THE HARE

back, run her foil and then make a prodigious leap sideways is a thing of common occurrence, but no artifice or stratagem is too unlikely for a hunted hare to attempt in the defeat of her pursuers.

CHAPTER IX

THE COUNTRY

Neighbouring Hunts, Owners and Tenants—Scratch Packs—Ownership—Nomenclature.

A PACK of beagles with no country to hunt over would not be of much use, so that before a hound has been acquired a locality must be found which is big enough to admit of two days a week without the same district being visited too often. This does not, of course, apply to anyone taking over an old-established country, but to the inauguration of a new pack in a locality where hare hunting is almost unknown.

The increase in popularity of foot beagles has led to many new packs being started and as there is every probability of more coming into existence, no apology is needed for giving a few hints to those who contemplate breaking fresh ground.

NEIGHBOURING HUNTS, OWNERS AND TENANTS

First and foremost it is necessary to find out if any hare-hunting pack claims a portion of the proposed terrain.

THE COUNTRY

To poach on ground that is already regularly hunted by a recognised pack is, of course, a very unsportsmanlike action.

When the locality is found to be free, the next thing to do is to ask the permission of landowners and occupiers, then with their consent the chief difficulty will be overcome. If a few of the principal landowners and farmers can be induced to form a hunt committee, it will be of great assistance to the master, and they will take a permanent interest in the fortunes of the pack.

If it is a country hunted by foxhounds the M.F.H. must then be consulted, but his permission is usually readily granted with the beagles master's undertaking not to disturb coverts.

Beagle meets should always be fixed for a district that foxhounds have visited a day or two previously and never just before they are expected there.

Hares seldom go into coverts with thick undergrowth, but they will occasionally and it is not always possible for the most energetic of whips to stop hounds. Should such a thing happen the master would do well to write at once to the M.F.H. and apologise.

A keeper who happened to be not too fond of foxes would be glad to lay the blame on the beagles for a blank draw. Foxes soon learn that beagles are not meant to hunt them, but they are not fond of hound smell near their usual kennel and the beagle master should get his pack out of a fox covert as quickly as possible.

The shooting tenant must be interviewed and the days he intends to shoot ascertained, so that the beagles will not be likely to disturb his ground previously.

The spread of towns into the country has driven many foxhound packs further afield, but domains thus bereft of hunting can in numerous instances be made available for hounds hunted on foot. Barbed wire fences and other obstructions to riding are by no means a handicap to those following beagles. The sporting inhabitants of towns and their suburbs can then enjoy an occasional day's hunting which is usually beyond their reach.

Because a man has been compelled by circumstances to dwell in a town or its vicinity it does not follow that he has not an innate love of the chase, and to individuals imbued with the right spirit the chance of a day's sport with the exercise accompanying it is a great boon.

The man who sets out to establish a new pack of hounds will doubtless be very keen on hunting and in all probability his actions will be governed

THE COUNTRY

by the desire to carry the horn; but however much he may spend himself in defraying the cost of the upkeep of hounds and other expenses of the hunt, he must remember the master is a public servant with duties to the country. It does not matter if he takes no subscription and runs the whole show out of his own pocket, landowners, farmers and residents in the district must all be considered. The mere fact that he and his hounds have taken over a certain portion of the country means that other packs are debarred, and people living in the district must put up with the sport he affords. Therefore he must arrange his days of meeting, and the time, to suit the majority. The meets may be advertised in the local papers, but cards should always be sent to landowners and occupiers in the locality that it is proposed to hunt.

SCRATCH PACKS

The indiscriminate starting of scratch packs just for temporary amusement should be discountenanced in these days, as they do a good deal of harm and bring well-organised hunts into discredit. The precedents and general rules of the M.F.H. Association might well be used as a guide to those who are thinking of starting beagles

THE ART OF BEAGLING

in a new country. Perhaps it ought to have been mentioned at the beginning that the man intending to hunt a country with a fresh pack should first of all apply to the Masters of Harriers and Beagles Association and find out if he will be infringing on the territory of any recognised hunt in the district he proposes to claim. If all is satisfactory he should then become a member of the Association after being duly proposed and seconded.

The owners of large estates occasionally encourage their youngsters in the love of hunting by giving them a few beagles, and such small beginnings have often helped to develop good sportsmen. Benefits derived from land, monetary or otherwise, are in these days very few and it would indeed be hard if the owner of many acres could not let his children hunt over them.

If the youngsters are born with the real spirit of the chase they will aspire later on to join a recognised pack, but in the beginning parents would do well to provide them with only small beagles, and confine their attention to rabbits. The latter when holes are stopped will afford very good sport.

The Eton beagles with those at Oxford and Cambridge have done much to foster the love of hunting. Many of the best amateur foxhound

(Upper) OVER THE PLOUGH
(Middle) OUT OF THE STUBBLE INTO THE ROOTS
(Lower) DOWN IN THE MARSH LAND

THE COUNTRY

huntsmen have graduated with beagles and there are people who insist that everyone should have followed on foot before being allowed to ride across country.

OWNERSHIP

Many of the present old-established packs have been built up solely by one man, which means that when he dies or gives up the country will be in chaos.

It is for this reason that when new packs are started the principle of having a hunt committee is strongly advocated.

Taxation, shortness of cash and the increased cost of keeping horses has limited the followers of foxhounds since the war to those with extra long purses. Consequently the number of people desiring to hunt with beagles is increasing daily and it looks as if very soon more packs will be wanted.

Now that hunting with foot beagles has become as firmly established as foxhounds it is more than ever imperative that countries should be under the control of hunt committees and the masters selected by them. Where hounds have been in existence for many years and are the property of the master it might be difficult to change, but a new country should most certainly be in the hands of a committee to manage. To ensure the hunt's success a large number of landowners and farmers should be asked to join in its support.

Hounds may belong to the master, but the country does not, and if a live committee is in existence they can take over control when there is a change of mastership.

Personally, I am all against hounds belonging to the country, because breeding and other matters connected with the pack must be left to the master who in a few years can entirely alter it—improve or spoil.

The committee could inform the new master the approximate height they preferred to have hounds, but the man's own preference for big or small would be certain to win in the end. Regimental colleges and school packs are on a different footing. The master, who usually acts as huntsman, is probably never in office for more than a couple of years and must be guided by the precedents of his predecessors. If he is a hound man he will try to maintain and possibly improve the pack by judicious breeding, but very often he has to depend on the kennelman for the characters of former hounds.

If every master before leaving was to set down

THE COUNTRY

in writing a faithful opinion of each hound and its work, a very useful record would be in existence for his successors to build on.

Cambridge having only one pack, the Trinity Foot, is therefore able to concentrate the assistance of all the University's hunting enthusiasts in its upkeep. Oxford has unfortunately two packs and the result is they have a hard struggle with expenses, much of which falls on the master. Both have nice-looking packs and give their followers excellent sport which is greatly to their credit, but I am hoping that some day they will overcome the present difficulties and combine. The matter must, however, be left to Oxford men to settle for themselves.

I look on both the Oxford and the Cambridge beagle packs as the means of fostering otherwise unsuspected hunting talent, also being schools for those who wish later on to start a fresh country.

NOMENCLATURE

It is a mistake to label a new pack with the master's name, even though it belongs to him, and it is much better to call it by a town or village in the centre of the hunt and by which it can be known for all time.

THE ART OF BEAGLING

If the newly exploited country is short of hares it can be restocked, and advice on that subject will be found in the chapter on the hare.

Do not despise a country because arable is in the ascendancy, for it can afford very good sport and is usually more frequented by hares than grass land.

CHAPTER X

THE HUNTSMAN AND HUNTING

Advice in the Field—Hallooing and Signals—Hunting Methods—The Kill—Recovering the Line—Picking out a Scent—Tricks of a Tired Hare—Casting and Lifting—Decisions and Conditions—Perseverance—Heads up.

ADVICE IN THE FIELD

IN most cases a master of beagles acts as huntsman, but when a professional is employed he should be given free scope to hunt, and never be interfered with or given advice in the field.

On the return to kennel, the master with some experience can discuss matters, get his huntsman's reasons for certain actions when in the performance of duties in the field, and if necessary take that opportunity of criticising, but it is a great mistake to interfere with or advise the man who is hunting hounds whilst thus employed. A huntsman's job is a one-man affair, and however indifferent he may be, he should be given free run to act in the way that appears best to him. Any suggestions when making a cast or at any time in the course of a run, even from the lips of the most expert, will do more harm than good.

The professional who has been promoted huntsman must have had some experience and qualifications or he would not have been given the post, so that it can be assumed that he knows something about the hare and her ways, with also the advantage over outside critics of knowing his hounds. Every huntsman worth his salt weaves for himself a hare's probable line of flight and her subsequent actions under certain conditions. It is more or less an automatic and unconscious brain process, but a very delicate thread of thought which is easily broken by suggestions from others.

If the master is dissatisfied with his huntsman, the sooner he gets rid of him the better, but whilst he is in office he must be allowed to hunt hounds according to his own ideas.

There is also another point worth mentioning between the master and a professional huntsman, which is the importance of allowing the man to persevere with a beaten hare if there is reason to presume she is getting tired. To the ordinary spectator there may have appeared to be no line for some time, but to the huntsman who knows his hounds some of the most sagacious will have given

THE HUNTSMAN AND HUNTING

him hints which are indications of a faint trail still existing. At these periods a little patience and steady perseverance will frequently bring the run to a satisfactory finish. The master should therefore curb his desire to look for a fresh hare and give his huntsman ample time either to work out the problem or to confess himself beaten.

The huntsman to a pack of foot beagles has a distinct advantage if he is a good runner, as he can then generally see which hounds are carrying the line and what has happened when they come to a check; but perhaps it is more important that he should be a good stayer rather than fast. The field can run when they can feel that way inclined and take it easy at other times, but a huntsman must always be on the move from the moment a hare is started until the end of the day. With a very moderate scent and the hare frequently viewed, the man-hunting hounds will often have more to do than on other occasions. Whilst hounds are running they are better left alone, and a huntsman should be content with keeping them in sight.

HALLOOING AND SIGNALS

A halloo is a very useful aid at times, but as a rule more time is lost in going to halloos than is gained. There is always danger of being hallooed on to a fresh hare, but besides that, if hounds are lifted they invariably take a few seconds before settling down again. This is more likely to occur with a thoroughly beaten hare, as the scent then is very slight and transitory, so that a pack which has its attention diverted from the line to which it was glued, may have much difficulty in owning it again, even though much nearer the hare. It is this period of the chase, both with hare-hounds and foxhounds, that has proved fatal and saved the life of the hunted one. The huntsman is then, of course, very keen on a kill and his natural excitement is liable to rise to the surface, but unless he curbs his feelings and allows no trace of them to appear in his voice or actions, he will convey his exuberance to hounds, when they will have their heads in the air instead of on the ground.

HUNTING METHODS

Different methods are permissible on different occasions and there can be no rule laid down, but with a tired hare it is generally better not to lift hounds whilst they can hunt until they can be given a view, which must bring the run to a finish. Hares vary considerably in their strength

THE HUNTSMAN AND HUNTING

and powers of endurance, but it should not be forgotten that the majority are capable of a burst of speed for a short distance when apparently dead beat.

When hounds under 14 inches are out of blood, that is have not accomplished a kill, on the last **four** occasions when hunted, the huntsman has then to work very hard in the final stages of a run. Whilst scent is good the pack will run with all its accustomed dash and keenness, when the huntsman has little to do except watch closely and be near at hand. At the moment, however, when the hare begins to tire, and as I have said, scent changes, hounds will still puzzle out the line and plod on, but, although their quarry may only be hopping along in front, they will be losing distance every moment. From want of previous success they fail to appreciate that the change indicates a tiring hare, and the result is that instead of driving on to a certain kill their speed slackens.

This is the moment when the huntsman must be ready to run and use all his skill to assist. Whilst things are going well it is perhaps better a huntsman should keep his mouth closed, but at this critical period, if a reliable member of the pack can speak to the line, it will infuse fresh life into the others to cheer them on to him. Although on these occasions it is permissible to take every advantage of the hunted one, a huntsman should try, if possible, to let hounds think they are doing it all themselves.

If there are two good whips who can run, they may be sent on ahead to watch the hare, keeping well on either side of her, so that they can see where she turns or squats. Should she do the latter, they must be careful not to disturb her. There must be no hallooing and only signals. It is then for the huntsman to decide what he will do, but it is usually advisable to reduce the gap and get on better terms. As I have said, a very tired hare will frequently show an amazing burst of speed and though jumping up in front of hounds may outdistance them to the first fence. Therefore, should the huntsman make up his mind to lift the pack to where she has squatted, it would be well for one of the whips to go still farther ahead and watch for any tricks she may perform when she imagines herself out of sight. A fox is a wily animal and has many dodges to escape pursuit, but is a fool compared to the hare in that respect.

If the hunted hare who has squatted is really tired, when put up she will make her effort and will creep into a fence or hide the moment hounds lose view, where she may never be discovered.

THE HUNTSMAN AND HUNTING

Excitable members of the field who happen to discover the hiding-place will then try to help with yells and other noises. These should be severely discouraged and after the spot has been indicated to the huntsman, everyone should stand perfectly still. As I have said, the idea is to make hounds think they are doing it all themselves, and though a beaten hare gives off practically no scent when squatting, they should be encouraged to find her even though she is plainly visible to human eyes. In spite of scientists who argue otherwise, I am firmly convinced animals have reasoning powers and the hound that discovers a tired hare squatting in a hedgerow or elsewhere, will remember it for a future occasion. I am not certain about other beasts or birds, but I am sure hounds and horses have very good memories.

THE KILL

Having brought the run to a satisfactory finish, it may be as well here to emphasise the importance of allowing the pack to tear and eat the body occasionally without touching it, more particularly when they are out of blood. At the same time you can blow your horn and encourage them with your voice. This is about the only period in a hunt that the loud-tongued cheer can do no harm. Unless you are on the spot some zealous member of the field will probably try to take the hare away from hounds, and when you want to secure mementoes of the run it may be done. You should, however, remember that hounds lose much of their interest and keenness in accomplishing a kill

IN FULL CRY

the moment you touch the hare. Let them think they have done it all themselves without any assistance from you.

A good pack that has been accounting for its hares regularly will require little aid from the huntsman and is more likely to succeed if not interfered with.

The reputation of a huntsman should rest on the performances of his hounds and not on his ability or science in assisting them. The man who depends mainly on his own cleverness in unravelling the

THE HUNTSMAN AND HUNTING

tangled puzzle a hare has set him will frequently find himself at a loss, and his hounds will gradually lose confidence in themselves as well as in their mentor.

RECOVERING THE LINE

A huntsman should be able to trust his hounds and he cannot do that or find the better qualities of each individual unless he allows them ample time to hunt and puzzle out the line. The merit or faults of a hound cannot be ascertained when the policy is pursued of lifting and casting at every check. The pack should always be given the opportunity of recovering the line on its own initiative and only when it fails in that object may the huntsman try his hand.

PICKING OUT A SCENT

There are exceptions to this rule, such as when sheep have foiled the line and a cast forward will mean clean ground, but even then if one hound has a sufficiently keen nose to pick out the scent through the sheep stain, it is better to leave them alone. If it is a grazing country the smelly muttons will often be encountered, and when hounds acquire the habit of sticking to the hunted animal's scent through conflicting odours, they are much less likely to check.

If a bad scenting bit of plough intervenes, either very dry or equally wet, and beyond is good turf, it is very tempting to lift hounds on to where more favourable conditions are likely to prevail. It can be argued that much time would be saved, but it is doubtful if any advantage would be gained supposing the hounds could carry the line at even a moderate pace. You must remember that if a pack is never permitted to pick out a scent under difficulties, it will soon lose the power of accomplishing that feat.

Then unless the huntsman is an exceptionally good runner he will not be able to go very fast over the plough.

If there is any delay in the early stages of a run whilst the hare is still comparatively fresh and therefore likely to forge ahead of her pursuers, it is permissible to lift on to better ground.

TRICKS OF A TIRED HARE

When, however, the hare is tired, she will probably take advantage of that bad scenting-ground to make her double, or practise the favourite trick of going a hundred yards into the

(*Upper*) DRAWING IN THE ROUGH
(*Lower*) CASTING OVER PLOUGH

(*Upper*) DRAWING UP TO THE HARE OVER MEADOWLAND
(*Lower*) LIFTING HOUNDS ONTO THE HARE

field, then turn back to run her foil to where she entered before starting off at right angles.

Let us imagine this is what has occurred. The field, three hundred yards across has been steam-cultivated and there is consequently no furrow. Hounds having been running over the grass naturally reduce their pace but carry on until they reach the spot where the hare turned. The older and more experienced may show a desire to hunt back, which is sure to be frustrated by a too officious whip crying " ware heel," or scent will be totally obliterated by the followers having run directly in the pack's wake.

CASTING AND LIFTING

The huntsman sees a good scenting area ahead, and hounds being at fault he lifts them over that two hundred yards of sticky plough, reasoning that if the hare has not gone on she has squatted in the field where he can return later to refind her. It will be seen that in this instance he would be wrong and the time lost in making the cast would jeopardise his chance of recovering the line of the hunted hare.

The novice—and it is to him principally these pages are addressed—may be unfamiliar with the terms " casting " and " lifting," so that a word of explanation may not be out of place.

" Casting " is drawing the hounds on with their heads down and trying all the ground as they go for the lost scent. They should be given plenty of time in the process and not be hurried on by whips.

" Lifting " either to a halloo or fresh ground is when the huntsman gathers the pack together without permitting any trying by the way and takes it direct to the spot indicated by individual hallooing or to where it is hoped to strike the line again.

Having taken hounds some distance away from the spot where they were last able to own the scent, the huntsman must use his own ingenuity to set them going again. The possibility of the hare having squatted in the plough will remain in his mind, but if that has happened she is unlikely to move, and beyond leaving someone to watch, he will try elsewhere first. A wide swing to right or left, whichever appears most likely, may result in hitting off the line where the hare left the headland of the arable field, but scent would then be very faint and the chances of a kill small.

The master should endeavour to make his

followers realise that it is opposed to all principles of hunting to run directly in the wake of the

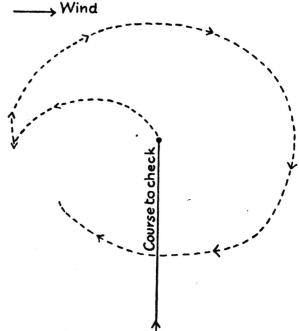

Method of casting at check. First Cast short and up wind; then down wind longer; but when a hare has been running a left or right ring she usually continues in that direction.

hounds as, apart from the hare's habit of running her foil, it tends to press them on at a check.

Before quitting the subject of lifting hounds, it may be as well to discuss it a little further. In foxhunting it is an established rule to cast forward first and give your fox the credit of going on. Hares are more liable to turn short, double back or go off at a right angle, but in spite of the difference I rather think the forward cast is best when hunting them. As I have said, the less beagles are lifted the better, but when it appears necessary, a cast forward will ensure keeping on terms with a travelling hare, and you can go back if not successful. The twisting hare will seldom go far before squatting, whereas the other sort will keep steadily on and be miles ahead if there is a lengthy check.

When you do make up your mind to lift hounds get on with the job quickly. A huntsman should be quick but never in a hurry. At the point where you hope to hit the line again, the pack should be allowed time to put their heads down, and the whip ought to give them plenty of room. If it is a moderate scenting day, hounds may not readily stoop after being lifted. Every huntsman, however experienced and clever he may be, is bound to be wrong occasionally in his calculations as to what the hare has done, but he should endeavour to make as few mistakes as possible. A pack will remember from previous experience that if lifted it will be to a spot where scent is more favourable and will be eager to search when the huntsman

THE HUNTSMAN AND HUNTING

encourages it to try. Two or three failures may be forgiven, but after that hounds will begin to lose confidence in the man and will be half-hearted in looking for the missing clue. Mutual confidence and understanding between the two is difficult to define, but unless it exists they will not work in perfect harmony without which all their efforts will be in vain.

DECISIONS AND CONDITIONS

Although a huntsman should have confidence in himself he should be without conceit and always ready to learn. No matter how old a man may be, or how long he has hunted, he will still have something to learn up to the day he dies. We may all be imbued with a certain amount of harmless conceit, but the man who allows that weakness to delude him into thinking he knows everything about hunting, is riding blindfold for a fall.

A little knowledge may be a dangerous thing, but a little experience is quite likely to lead us into making mistakes. Those who have either hunted the hare a few times or watched others will frequently lay down the law as to what that animal is likely to do or has done. In spite of over thirty years' experience I must confess that it has not

THE ART OF BEAGLING

taught me what tricks a hare will play on any subsequent occasion. Keepers and others who have opportunities of watching a hare in her idle moments or when she has been coursed by a cur are usually very emphatic as to the exact line that she will take with hounds. If not previously hunted that particular hare may fulfil their predictions for a preliminary ring, but when once realising she is being hunted by scent, inherited instincts acquired in several hundred years will come into play and then no man can foretell her further movements.

A hare having a very keen sense of smell and realising at once she is hunted by her scent, will endeavour to shake off her pursuers by running over ground the least likely to retain that scent. The road is one of her most favoured places for this purpose and she may run it for a mile or more before turning off. Unless there is a road hound of proved ability, the huntsman will then find himself in difficulties.

When there are no indications to inform the huntsman in which direction the hare turned, he will more or less be left to guess at what has happened. When this situation occurs the field should not be allowed on the road until the hounds have felt for the scent, when, if there is no real road hound, the wiseacres of the pack will give

THE HUNTSMAN AND HUNTING

some signs of the direction the hare has taken. When the huntsman has satisfied himself in which direction to proceed, he can walk smartly along the road, pausing at each smeuse and gateway to give hounds a chance, or if there is grass on either side, time can be saved by making good both sides at once. The huntsman can then run on at a fair pace and hit the scent before it gets cold or evaporates.

This method answers very well if the hare, after running a certain distance on the road, turns off into the fields without playing any tricks, but frequently she will take this opportunity to practise some of those artful wiles which lead to a huntsman's confusion.

Sometimes she will run for half a mile on a road, turn off through a gateway and run a hundred yards into an open field, when she will turn round to run her foil back to the gateway and continue on the road.

The followers will naturally think all is plain sailing again, and in their eagerness not to be left behind will effectually obliterate the scent left by the hare on her return. In a case of this kind the huntsman has generally to acknowledge defeat, as by the time he realises what has happened, scent will have practically disappeared.

When a really tired hare takes to the road the huntsman should proceed with more caution, as if there is a fairly thick hedge on either side she is very likely to lie up in it, making a big jump to avoid leaving any trace to her hiding-place. The distance an apparently thoroughly beaten hare can leap would be almost unbelievable except to those who have seen the feat performed.

It may be accepted as a rule with few exceptions that before a hare squats, either in a strange place or going to her usual form, she will make several turns, never making straight for the spot she intends finally to occupy. Thus if hounds on getting on to some plough, run up one furrow, down another, and follow an erratic sort of line across, you may be pretty certain the hare has either squatted, or had thought of doing so. However, it sometimes happens that the cry of hounds in the near distance will induce her to change her plans. The huntsman would therefore be wise to make sure she has not gone on before making a systematic search of the plough.

The well-known trick of a tired hare pushing another out of its form and usurping the seat left vacant is responsible for many unavoidable changes and leaves the huntsman guessing why the hunt is unduly prolonged.

THE HUNTSMAN AND HUNTING

The change from the hunted animal on to one that is fresh is the rock that usually wrecks a huntsman's hope of success both in pursuit of fox and hare, but it happens more frequently with the latter. Hounds that have been killing with fair regularity are less likely to change than others.

The reason for this is that every hare has its own distinctive smell, which though very slight, is sufficient for a pack to distinguish when it has found by experience that by sticking to the original scent a kill is more likely to be attained. This acquired habit of remaining faithful to the line of the animal first started is of the utmost importance in all hunting and should be encouraged as much as possible.

The stoat would never achieve a kill if he allowed the scent of other rabbits to lure him from the line of the one he was hunting. The same holds good with the various wild animals that live by hunting, and we may conclude the " no change " system was a part of the gift with which nature originally endowed her hunters. The fact that hounds of to-day have in a great measure lost this valuable attribute is probably our fault and the way we have handled them. The instinct is doubtless still there if we can only bring it to life again and cultivate it properly.

THE ART OF BEAGLING

More hares are lost by going to halloos than are killed by those means, but still I do not wish to infer you should never go to one. A halloo may occasionally prove very useful when hounds are at fault, but as long as they can hunt it is generally safest to leave them alone.

When anyone gives you information as to where the hare has gone, whether it is one of your field or a stranger, always thank them civilly, but act on your own judgment about making use of what has been supplied. Trust your hounds first, even before the most reliable member of the field.

The average individual will very seldom be able to tell you exactly where he saw the hare and he will usually have looked away before she finally disappeared, so that if she changes her direction he will be unable to tell you. The man viewing a hare at close quarters should remain perfectly still and watch her closely, at the same time observing her pads to see if they show any signs of mud. In this way he will be able to tell if she has been hunted and by her general movements how tired she may be. If frightened she will, for the moment, shed all appearance of fatigue and appear quite fresh.

For some reason that has never been fully explained, both the fox and the hare appear to

(*Upper*) THE KILL
(*Lower*) THE WORRY

THE HUNTSMAN AND HUNTING

hold their scent when suddenly frightened. Being chased by a cur is a frequent cause of the animal's scent disappearing, but how much of this is due to the smell of the cur and how much to being frightened I have never been able to decide.

As advice to the individual viewing a hare and on his subsequent information of the fact to the huntsman, I should say " state exactly the place you saw her last and *not* where you imagined she was going."

PERSEVERANCE

Don't lose faith in your hounds because they run round giving tongue on newly seeded ground that was subject to a sharp morning frost, which has since been melted by the sun. The hare whilst feeding overnight had her scent frozen up in the drops of moisture hanging to the leaves and the morning sun has released it.

My advice to the huntsman is, never to give up persevering if a hare has been run any time and there is the faintest vestige of scent left.

HEADS UP

As additional advice let me repeat what has already been written, namely the importance of doing nothing to get hounds' heads up with a beaten hare. Scent then has changed and weakened, but though the older hounds may be able to detect the faint line, any halloo or interruption will break the fragile thread that connects them with their hare. Once get their heads up and they will never recover the elusive clue.

At this time it is, therefore, of the utmost importance to keep perfectly quiet. A halloo or cheer should never be used then unless the pack can be actually given a view of the beaten hare.

CHAPTER XI

THE WHIPPER-IN

Obedience to the Huntsman—Carrying a Whip—Counting the Pack—Position—Damage to Property—Stopping Riot—Rating—The Noisy Whip—Exercising—The Young Hound.

THE above title is correct, but custom of late years has brought into general use an abbreviation and the individual assisting with a pack is now called a " Whip."

OBEDIENCE TO THE HUNTSMAN

The majority of beagle packs depend almost entirely on the services of amateurs who work very hard at what is often a thankless task. Frequently it happens that a man is asked to take on the job on account of his running abilities and without any previous knowledge of hounds or hunting. To these a few hints on a whip's duties may prove useful, but at the same time it may be as well to add that nearly every huntsman has his own ideas of what his assistant should or should not do. Whether the ideas are right or wrong matters not, the whip must obey orders from the man hunting hounds, as otherwise there would be hopeless confusion.

CARRYING A WHIP

Some packs are blessed or perhaps cursed with four or five whips, but personally I think there should never be more than two, or at the most three, to act regularly. Although it is not a general custom I think the master would do well to ask certain members of his field, men who understand hunting, to carry a whip, as there are many occasions when they could make themselves useful if they had that article in their hands, but without it are powerless to assist. These men would, of course, not be expected to exert themselves or keep on terms with the pack, nor would they be looked on as whips, but if at any time they happened to be in a position to give their services, the lash and thong affair would enable them to act promptly.

There are many things that may occur in the course of a day's hunting ; hounds may strike heel-way on being lifted to a halloo or when cast ; the least riotous pack may be tempted to err when a rabbit gets up under their noses. A fresh hare

THE WHIPPER-IN

may jump up in the middle of a run at a critical moment, and it might happen to be necessary to stop hounds going into a covert or entering a forbidden area. In all these cases the crack of a whip at the head of the pack, before it was in full swing, would do the trick, whereas running behind and rating has little effect.

Any man, however slow a runner he may be, is likely to find himself in the position to act on these occasions. The fact that a member of the hunt who was not an official had been asked by the master to carry a whip would be a recognition of his general hunting knowledge.

I should also like it to be an understood thing that any master of beagles visiting another pack should carry his whip. On the few occasions on which I do hunt with another pack I am very careful not to carry a whip, lest my services should be requisitioned for a burst of speed which would be beyond my powers. This, however, need not apply to the active and energetic master in the full vigour of youth.

COUNTING THE PACK

After this digression let us return to the whips proper and their duties. Perhaps the first thing to

THE ART OF BEAGLING

learn is to count the pack and to do it at frequent intervals of the day, more particularly when there are several hares afoot. Hounds should always be counted by couples, single ones reckoning as a half. It is not an easy matter for the huntsman as the hounds are probably all round him, but the whip on one side will not find it difficult after a little practice.

The subject of drawing has been attended to and the various methods of different huntsmen. I can only repeat that my preference is for hounds to draw for their hare and only when they are very scarce do I want the field to beat the ground.

POSITION

Hounds should be allowed to range fairly wide and when there are two whips one should be on either flank, and if there is a third he can be in close attendance on the huntsman.

The whips should be informed on starting the line of country to be drawn, but circumstances may make it necessary to alter this as the huntsman will often get indications from his old hounds that a hare has been feeding and give a pointer to where she has gone to her seat.

In the early part of the season before the young

entry have learnt their business, the whips have to be particularly alert, more so with the hounds that have hunted at walk as they are liable to have acquired independent habits which must be curbed at once. If it is a grazing country a flock of sheep may excite the young hounds to give chase, and any such desire should be promptly nipped in the bud.

Should any fox coverts be in the district the whips must be careful to see hounds do not enter, and also coverts that are sacred to pheasants. It is very seldom that a fox will leave a covert when beagles are in the district, as he knows he is in no danger when he hears no tramp of horses' feet. The vibrations of sound through the earth convey messages to the wild of things that are happening some distance away. Instinct undoubtedly teaches some animals to interpret this " wireless " system of communication, but it is only the older and more experienced that are able by reasoning to recognise sounds that signal danger.

Foxes may pay little heed to the cry of beagles when hunted afoot and running within the neighbourhood of their lairs, but they have a great dislike to the smell of any dog within the boundaries of coverts which they consider their home, so that it behoves the officials attending beagles to see there is no violation of those sacred precincts.

The pheasant also is a very knowing bird and quickly realises that although hounds may disturb him, that he is in no danger, but he also has a habit of straying on to other properties, and as the shooting owner desires to keep him at home, any wood or covert devoted to pheasants should be carefully avoided.

DAMAGE TO PROPERTY

All hunting, whether it be riding to foxhounds or running to beagles, should be based on a consideration for others that do not participate in the sport, but who often suffer annoyance therefrom. The whips are the master's assistants and they should always be on the look-out to help him in minimising the annoyance or damage to those over whose land the hunt proceeds. It is the obliteration of self and the consideration for the feelings of others that marks a good sportsman and a gentleman. In the hectic enjoyment of the moment when hounds are running we are all apt to forget those to whom we owe our pleasure.

Therefore, apart from all other duties to hounds the whips should ever have in their minds the interests of farmers, landowners, and shooting tenants. The master hunting hounds himself is

THE WHIPPER-IN

fully occupied in that task and cannot see what is going on behind him.

When a huntsman has the full confidence of his hounds it is very seldom he has need of a whip in making a cast and the less those individuals are in evidence the better. The pack may swing a little wider than the huntsman requires and he may wish the half-circle to be somewhat more restricted, when a whip can make it bend in the requisite direction; but there should be as little noise as possible.

A whip may have a good voice, but he should exercise a great restraint in its use and also be equally sparing in cracking the instrument of torture he carries in his hand. The nervous or shy hound may have his attention arrested and diverted at a critical moment on hearing a whip cracked.

Whilst hounds are running hard with a fairly good scent they may take little heed of extraneous noises, but at a check or when puzzling out a faint line, the slightest sound may distract them and the thread broken then may never again be mended This is the time when the whips should keep their mouths closed and eyes and ears wide open. The field, seeing there is a break in the run and hounds are no longer giving tongue, will usually start coffee-housing, but you as a whip are an official of the hunt and must not let yourself be lured from duty.

STOPPING RIOT

In stopping hounds from running riot, rabbits or other forbidden game, the whip must get to their heads, as it is useless rating them from behind. This is a moment when you may crack your whip and if you can reach the leading miscreant you may give him a smart cut with the lash. Should a rabbit get up, place yourself immediately in the path it ran and then you will be able to nip in the bud the desire of any hounds to pursue. However, in the matter of administering punishment you should get definite instructions from the huntsman. Unless you know all the hounds you may perchance hit a trusted old veteran who, feeling guiltless of wrongdoing, does not take the trouble to get out of the way. Then in the early part of the season you should deal gently with the young hounds which, having little experience of hare, put their heads down to a rabbit's scent and perhaps give tongue. It is, of course, important they should be taught that rabbits are not allowed, but it is essential they should learn to use their noses, and if rated too severely may think it is

THE WHIPPER-IN

for using them and not realise it is because that particular scent is forbidden.

When the huntsman is making a cast I have seen whips flogging hounds on to him and not allowing them a moment to get their heads down. When this happens the pack may pass over the scent without noticing it. In casting, a well-trained pack is best left alone by the whips and will swing themselves in front of their huntsman with a wave of his hand.

Lifting is, however, a different matter. The huntsman wants to get hounds off their noses for the moment and take them to more favourable ground. It may be that sheep have stained the soil, or a bit of sticky plough with promise of grass beyond; or, again, it might be the hare had been viewed, all of which are reasons for the desire to lift. The whip must then put hounds on to the huntsman and not allow them to linger, but it should be done without rating and as little whip-cracking as possible.

Hounds know how far they have carried the scent and they are doing no wrong in trying to puzzle it out, so that if rated then they may refuse to persevere on a future occasion. A hound should never be rated unless he commits some offence. In all cases the punishment should fit the crime, whether it be by whip-lash or the tone of the voice. This is only common sense and the man who desires to become an official whip should reason it out for himself.

RATING

Hounds should not look on a whip as an individual from whom they must flee in mortal terror, but as a friend who is there to assist in catching the hare and who is only to be feared on the occasion of a lapse into sin.

Should a hound refuse to obey the huntsman's voice after a third call the whip should go swiftly and silently behind the disobedient one until near enough to give him a smart cut with the lash. If it is intended to hit an offender it is useless yelling at him first as he knows what to expect and will take care to get out of the way. When a huntsman uses his voice to recall a hound to his side, a whip ought never to repeat the command and his duty is to see the command obeyed.

It is a hard and fast rule in the management of hounds to punish first and rate afterwards. Also if a whip should find it necessary to go after a transgressor with intent to punish and fail to get within striking distance, he must never hit the culprit after he gets back to the huntsman.

THE WHIPPER-IN

There are certain deadly sins, such as chasing sheep, which do not admit of any leniency and the only cure is a sound flogging. When caught in the act the delinquent should be coupled to a post or rail and grasping his stern in one hand, the necessary strokes can be given with the other.

Personally, I think this should be done by the huntsman as he knows best how much each particular hound can stand. After such punishment it is sometimes advisable to couple the hound up to another for a short time or otherwise he may run away.

These necessary acts of correction are best done in private with no field looking on, but a flagrant case cannot be passed over and the punishment must be administered at once. It is better if the huntsman and whips can have a few mornings to themselves before the season starts so that the pack has learnt more or less to behave when there is an audience to see it.

The young entry, in addition to their initiation to hunting, have to be taught certain things, and when a fairly large number has been put on, two whips are of great assistance to the huntsman. In fact two efficient whips are of more use the first month of the season than all the rest of the time. Discipline to some extent may be instilled during the summer and conditioning period, but the excitement engendered by hearing the older hounds giving tongue may excite the novices to acts of insubordination.

When the huntsman in making a cast desires the pack to swing to a narrower circle than they are doing, the whip must keep on the outside of them and make the leading hounds bend in the required direction. This should be done as quietly as possible without any fuss or rating and no whip cracking. The pack has done nothing wrong, only taken a rather wider sweep than the huntsman thinks necessary, led perhaps by an overkeen and ambitious hound.

THE NOISY WHIP

A noisy whip is an abomination and is frequently responsible for hounds getting their heads up at a moment when all their powers should be concentrated on holding the line. The man who wishes to become a first-class whip should endeavour to do all his work without raising his voice much above a whisper and as hounds have very sensitive hearing it is quite possible. A pack that has confidence in its huntsman will always be on the alert for his voice and when others halloo or make noises it only causes confusion.

THE WHIPPER-IN

However indifferent a huntsman may be the whip should never attempt to usurp his functions, but should remain a loyal adherent, profiting by his mistakes and acquiring thereby wisdom for the day when he shall carry the horn.

There are sure to be occasions when the huntsman, however good a runner, may not be up when hounds check, and it is a tempting moment for a whip to try his hand. Unless the hare—unmistakably the run one—is viewed, a whip had much better leave hounds alone and let them recover the line unaided. A pack that has been accustomed to be handled by one man will not follow very readily another, and even should the whip succeed in his cast, he will probably only get half the pack on the line.

The nearer hounds can keep to their hare the more likely will the scent hold good, so that there is some excuse for the whip who takes on the huntsman's duties when that individual is absent. It should, however, be remembered that frequently more time is lost by casting hounds than allowing them to recover the line themselves, and in the latter case when they succeed they will be less likely to check again.

Whatever the circumstances, and however much a whip may feel he knows the direction the hare has taken, he is never justified in interfering until hounds have given up trying and are at a total loss. Even in the latter case he would perhaps act wisely by standing perfectly still and allowing more time for the old hounds to try back. When the young and enterprising portion of the pack fail to hit the line forward, it is pretty nearly certain the hare has doubled short back and if the field can be persuaded to be quiet the veterans will solve the puzzle.

The whip who is always looking for opportunities to hunt the pack himself is disloyal to the huntsman and will do more harm than good. In his efforts to help the pack he will frequently be lifting it on to fresh hares and thereby endangering the " non-changing " quality of its work.

There are some hounds that inherit the ability of sticking to one hare, but as a rule it is acquired by practice and the success attending it. Every hare has its own particular and distinctive smell, so that when a pack realises that by sticking to one scent it is more likely to kill, it is on the right way to acquire the habit. It is also a habit that is soon lost when hounds are being continually hallooed on to fresh hares.

With the majority of beagle packs the huntsman depends for assistance on amateur whips, men who

THE WHIPPER-IN

give their services for the love of sport, but if they agree to undertake the duties they should try to be as efficient as if they were professionals.

It is essentially a job for a young man as on occasions it entails much hard work and good running powers, though a huntsman should always remember his whips are volunteers and be considerate in his demands on their services.

EXERCISING

The man who desires to become a real efficient whip to a pack of hounds ought to spend some of his summer days in the kennel and help exercise. Thereby he will be able to learn the names of hounds and get an insight into the character of each.

THE YOUNG HOUND

If the young entry put on is fairly large there are certain to be some with an inclination to chase sheep or fowls ; a desire to be promptly nipped in the bud. It is on these occasions that the amateur whip can be of great assistance to a master who hunts the pack. When possible advantage should be taken of the summer months to let hounds see sheep and fowls, when any individual showing a sign of chasing should be given a severe lesson.

THE ART OF BEAGLING

The punishment should be followed with a rating of "ware sheep" or "ware," whatever the culprit has chased. In this way when the necessary discipline has been instilled during the summer, the pack start their hunting season without being guilty of any bad breaks. At the same time on a first morning the whips should be on either flank ready to stop a hound showing signs of misbehaviour. The whip should realise that when the young hounds hear the others give tongue for the first time they know something is being hunted, but not having put their heads down do not know what it is.

Should a flock of sheep then wheel across the line, the youngsters may think they are joining in the chase of mutton. Prompt action by the assistant on the flank can stop pursuit before it becomes serious, for if such a chase is allowed to continue any distance without reproof, there is grave danger of the culprits acquiring the habit. Another little matter for the whip is when he notices a young hound putting its nose down to a scent other than a hare and perhaps giving tongue. He should remember a hound's nose is given it to distinguish the various scents and before it is entered to hare it cannot know that either rabbit, pheasant or partridge are forbidden

THE WHIPPER-IN

game. By all means let a young hound use its nose and then when properly entered to hare is time enough to make it understand all other scents are " riot." This is perhaps a matter belonging to the huntsman's province, but he may be forward with the older hounds and the duty of stopping the youngster devolves on the whip. The delinquent must, of course, be stopped and not allowed to continue with the scent it has found, but the rating should be of a mild character or the puppy will think he is not allowed to use his nose.

I have seen whips rate old hounds very severely for putting their heads down to other scents than a hare's, although they did not give tongue. This is, of course, quite wrong as they are only investigating the nature of the scent, and unless they speak to it should certainly not be reproved.

CHAPTER XII

THE FIELD

Subscription and Ownership of Packs—Hunt Uniform—Followers' Kit—Importance of Footwear—Consideration and Care against Damage—Fitness—Hound Pace and Man Pace—Human Scent—Position—Hound Identification—Rules to Follow in the Field—Sympathy with the Hound.

THE man of experience with hounds and hunting will, of course, understand that any suggestions set down in this last chapter are not meant for him, but for the follower, for many people come out with beagles having little or no previous knowledge of the sport.

Masters, huntsmen, and whips must naturally be in a minority of those interested in following foot beagles, so that no further apology is needed for devoting a full chapter for " the good of the greater number." For insignificant details which may appear to the initiated as hardly worth mentioning will possibly prove useful to the less experienced.

Anyone with the love of sport born in them and insufficient means or riding ability to follow foxhounds should try to join a pack of beagles. The little hounds have become deservedly popular

THE FIELD

of late years, and in most parts of the country there are regular established packs hunting on certain recognised days. Formerly anyone with a little land would start a scratch pack and hunt at any odd time, but these attempts are now generally discouraged and each hunt has its own well-defined area.

SUBSCRIPTION AND OWNERSHIP OF PACKS

The majority of packs are more or less supported by subscriptions, which is a good thing as it gives the contributors an interest in the hunt and also obliges the master to consider the wishes of his field. There are probably few packs that rely for their support entirely on subscriptions and the master has generally to shoulder the bulk of the expenses, but then, for that privilege, he enjoys the honour of his position, and also, probably, the pleasure of hunting hounds. Foxhound masters have to suffer in the same way and those who accept the responsibilities of a fashionable country have usually to dip pretty deeply into their pockets, whilst they are not even allowed to hunt hounds. Beagle masters enjoying this privilege must, therefore, be content to pay for this pleasure.

Most beagle packs are the property of the various

masters, the Worcester Park and the West Surrey being the only exceptions I can recall at the moment. The objection to hounds being the property of the hunt is that although a master may take over a first-rate working pack, he may in a few years lose all those valuable qualities in order to achieve some craze for make, shape or colour.

My own opinion is that it would in all cases be better if the incoming master took over the pack at a valuation, or, if that arrangement was unsatisfactory, the hounds could be sold at public auction. Breeders have all their little peculiarities and many, I regret to say, in selecting those hounds from which they intend to breed, think more of good looks than the acid test of performances in the field. Then there is the question of height varying from 13 to 16 inches, and each individual has his own idea as to which shows the better sport, but that is a point the hunt committee would have to arrange with the new master and state definitely the standard to be maintained.

This is rather getting away from the subject of " The Field," but the future welfare of the pack is worth the consideration of those who follow it and as subscribers are usually entitled to a vote, they should give the matter careful thought.

THE FIELD

Age is no barrier to hunting with beagles, and although the man approaching his " threescore and ten " may find want of wind prevents him from doing much running, he can still see most of the sport by walking ; but it is more to the young that I speak.

The first thing to do is to find out the nearest pack with meets that are within reasonable distance, and then apply to master or secretary for permission to join. This is readily granted and, after a subscription has been paid, cards of fixtures, unless advertised, will be sent.

The amount of subscription is generally left to the individual with an average fixed minimum of about three guineas for members and two guineas for subscribers, and must depend to a certain extent on how much each can afford. As has already been stated the expense of maintaining a pack is very heavy, and the master has to find the balance. Therefore, those who enjoy the sport should not think how little they can give, but how much. Unless a pack is well fed, properly housed and efficiently looked after, it cannot be expected to hunt in a workmanlike manner or catch hares. Subscribers should remember that when fixture cards are sent, there is a certain expense in postage in addition to the trouble of writing. Both with foxhounds and beagles, subscriptions are supposed to be due at the beginning of the season, but it is an item that is often postponed to an unknown date.

Money is an uninteresting subject to write or talk about, but the sinews of sport must be maintained, and however long an old member may delay payment it is incumbent on the novice to stump up before he joins the hunt.

The majority of people nowadays have cars and they are certainly the most convenient means of attending meets, but the push bicycle is still available and is useful for those not possessing cars. Unless the distance of the meet permits of walking there, I strongly advise all beaglers to take with them a change of shoes and stockings. With a car it is advisable to take a complete change, as you never know how the day may turn out, and you may get soaked to the skin by the rain, or, if sufficiently keen, may swim a river, whilst there is always a chance of failing quite to clear a brook and falling back into the water. Any of these occurrences will leave you very uncomfortable and perhaps result in serious consequences if you have to drive back in wet clothes. Never mind how fine the morning, always be prepared for the worst.

THE FIELD

HUNT UNIFORM

Each hunt has its own uniform, and though clothes may not help to catch a hare, or be a guarantee of the pack's ability to hunt, it is only courteous to landowners and occupiers to turn out reasonably smart. The green coats and black caps should be worn solely by the huntsman and whips, and, of course, the master, if he is not acting as huntsman. Some hunts give a button to each subscriber or member and this seems an excellent plan. White breeches with stockings of the colour favoured by the particular hunt complete the outfit, but although none except actual officials should wear the green coat, there is no reason why others should not don white breeches, especially those who mean to run.

FOLLOWERS' KIT

In giving advice as to the most suitable clothes to wear, either to men or women followers, I feel a certain amount of hesitation, and can only suggest the outfit which in my long experience has proved suitable. Running shoes with spikes, shorts and a sweater are admirable for a run across country, but, except on occasional days, there are frequent checks when the field is asked to stand still, and a cold wind would quickly find its way through a sweater.

Then, as most people know, a spiked shoe is decidedly uncomfortable on macadam or tarmac. " Shorts " are also very nice for a straight-away run, as they give the knees perfectly free action, but there is no protection against thorns and briers, both of which are generally to be met with in a day's beagling. This scanty covering would also be found very inadequate on one of those days when the wind is in the east and rain turns to ice as it falls.

If you are really keen you would want to see a hunt to a finish whatever the weather was like, but it would rather spoil your pleasure should the run develop into a walk and your bare knees be exposed to the wintry blast.

IMPORTANCE OF FOOTWEAR

Let us begin at the bottom, then, and work upwards. Unless a man is such an expert runner that he can afford to handicap himself he would do well to be shod as lightly as possible. Remember the old saying that " a pound on the foot is a stone on the back." After trying many kinds of footwear I finally settled on light canvas with

THE FIELD

thin rubber soles known as " gym " shoes, and in America as " sneakers." Some of those who have tried them complain they quickly wear out, but as you can buy half a dozen pairs for ten shillings and that number will last a season they cannot be called expensive. With the thin rubber you can get a good grip on the ground and the mud does not cling to them like leather. The man who does not mean to attempt any running will naturally wear thick shooting boots or shoes. Another advantage of the light canvas footwear is that however wet they may get they quickly dry, and those who go beagling must expect to ford brooks or be up to the ankles in muddy gateways. The leather boot will stand a certain amount of moisture, but once the wet gets in over the top it keeps there for the rest of the day.

Woollen stockings, of course, and no matter how damp they become they keep warm whilst you are moving, but should you be persuaded to stop after a hunt for refreshment you must not sit in them or you will be certain to suffer later on. On occasions I have stopped for tea when walking home and with no change, I remove shoes, pull my stockings down and put my feet in the legs which are warm and dry. This is a tip worth remembering.

If it is the house of a comparative stranger and you do not feel like appearing without shoes with the feet of your stockings flapping about, take my advice and don't stop. Never sit with wet or damp feet is a golden rule for keeping clear of colds and other unpleasant ills.

I always wear a thin and very light woollen waistcoat and run with my coat open, which allows the air to circulate round the body. Then at a check or when hunting is slow, I button up the coat and do not feel the coldest wind. A light sweater should answer the same purpose, but a coat should be worn over it and, as I have said, unbuttoned whilst running. The ultra-smart young man will probably object to running with his coat flying open, as he will think it does not look well, but he should remember the difference between running and standing or walking is about equal to the change of temperature from a Turkish bath to a refrigerator. By all means turn out as smartly as possible; but do not sacrifice comfort and risk of health for the sake of appearances. I, however, think that the regular members of a hunt should be respectably clad out of respect to the master and out of courtesy to those over whose land you follow hounds.

I dare not advise what ladies should wear but

merely suggest they should follow on the lines set down for men. Nowadays women clothe themselves much more sensibly and there is no reason why girls who hunt regularly with beagles should not wear breeches and stockings.

It may seem I have gone rather too thoroughly into such an unimportant detail as clothes, but it is these small matters, the neglect of which may spoil our pleasure in a day's sport.

CONSIDERATION AND CARE AGAINST DAMAGE

Although the field must adhere to recognised rules of hunting and obey the master's behests, I should set down their first duty to be a thoughtful consideration for those over whose land they hunt. We are indebted to the courtesy of landlords and tenants for the privilege of following the hounds over their land, a privilege we should see is never abused. Unless a man is quite certain he can clear a fence he should never attempt jumping, and should he unwittingly break one, he ought to report it to the master or better still see the owner and offer to pay for its repair.

On coming to a gate that is closed it is better to climb over, and remember the man opening one is responsible for seeing it shut, no matter how many of the field are behind him. Much trouble and annoyance are caused the farmer when gates are left open so that sheep and cattle escape into other fields. Referring again to fences, that is thorn hedges, even a speedy repair of a breakage is not satisfactory to the occupier of land. A good farmer takes a pride in his fences and is naturally annoyed at finding several unsightly gaps in what was previously a neat hedge. The first person forcing himself through a hedge may not make much impression, but others are sure to follow and when the last of a big field goes through a permanent gap will be established. Therefore, whenever a gate or timber is handy, make use of them and thus avoid doing unnecessary damage. The huntsman and whips may have to keep in close touch with hounds, but the field are not obliged to follow in their footsteps.

Beagling is often carried on in the neighbourhood of towns, where there are usually numerous market gardens in which hares go to feed. A hare may be found elsewhere but she is pretty sure to run where she has fed overnight. There are young and tender plants in these gardens which would be ruined by being trampled on, so that on entering a market garden the field should stick to the paths, or if only a small place, keep outside altogether.

THE FIELD

In foxhunting everyone carries a whip, but with beagles it is not considered the thing for anyone to carry one unless at the master's request.

FITNESS

The man going out for his first day with beagles may decide beforehand that he will take it easy, but if the love of the chase is in his blood, the cry of hounds will fire him with the desire to be with them. Unless, then, he has kept himself fit with other exercise he is very liable to strain his heart by unaccustomed exertions and the middle-aged who has been a good runner in his youth is more likely to attempt a pace beyond his wind powers.

If, therefore, you are going to run, get yourself moderately fit before you attend a meet. With wind and leg muscles in good order, running after hounds is a pleasure, but otherwise it is apt to be labour and toil.

HOUND-PACE AND MAN-PACE

The mistake frequently made is in starting off at a fast pace—faster than it is possible to keep up. He who wants to see a hunt to a finish should begin slowly—well below his normal pace—and then, on getting his wind, he can go on without feeling any distress.

THE ART OF BEAGLING

In the first burst when the hare is found, hounds usually go away at a great pace and the best runners can seldom keep with them, but nine times out of ten there is soon a slowing down. My advice to the moderate runner is to take it easy at the start with a slow jog, listening carefully to hear which way hounds are turning and then keeping on the inside of the circle. Hares are supposed always to begin by making a circle, but it is not invariably the case. When hounds are up-wind of you it is easy to recognise in which direction they are heading, but if down-wind it is advisable to keep them within sight or they are easily lost. These hints are not meant for the really good runner who can go fast and stay, as he will never be far from the pack and has all the best of the fun.

The neophyte on seeing hounds start off with a burst of music when close to their hare, is apt to think that scent is a stable quality remaining for some time where left, and does not realise its volatile character or how easily it is affected by other extraneous smells. The individual may have grasped the fact that horses, cattle, sheep and manure-stained ground have a baleful influence on scent, but he usually fails to realise the strength of his own smell or its power in effacing the hare's faint perfume.

THE FIELD

HUMAN SCENT

If our detectives could cultivate the scenting abilities of hounds they would find it a much surer method of running criminals to ground than the finger-print system, for everyone has a distinctive smell of his or her own. Hounds are familiar with their huntsman's smell and consequently it does not bother them so much as would a stranger's. For this reason, it is important for followers to give the huntsman plenty of room and not walk after him whilst he is making a cast. Common sense will tell you that if your scent is stronger than a hare's it must do harm to walk over the line.

POSITION

The fast runner should remember never to run exactly in the wake of hounds, but a little to one side or the other, keeping a sharp look-out on the leaders of the pack and stopping instantly on the slightest sign of hesitation. Hares turn very short and when least expected, so that if not exercising great care, those a little too forward may find themselves over the line, and prevent a quick recovery.

THE ART OF BEAGLING

HOUND IDENTIFICATION

On your first day with the pack it is well to make the master's acquaintance at the meet as once hunting has commenced he will have little time for conversation. Should you intend to hunt with them regularly you will find that it adds to the pleasures of the chase if you can learn the names and identify the hounds, when it will be of greater interest to watch them at work and you will appreciate the abilities of individual hounds. A few Sundays spent in the kennel with the master's permission and under the kennelman's tutelage ought to make you familiar with different members of the pack.

RULES TO FOLLOW IN THE FIELD

There are certain well-known rules in hunting which those who have spent their lifetime at the sport imagine everyone must know, but the beginner I am hoping to initiate into the mysteries will probably have never heard of them. Let us, therefore, jot down a few for his instructions.

Stand still at a check and do not talk. Never run in the wake of hounds if at all near them, but

(*Upper*) THE HUNT IN PROGRESS, SHOWING CORRECT POSITION OF WHIPS AND FIELD
(*Lower*) THROUGH THE ROOTS

(*Upper*) CHANGING GROUND
(*Lower*) A WATER OBSTACLE

THE FIELD

on one side or the other. Don't halloo, but hold up your cap if you see the hare, and the huntsman can then please himself what he does. If a hare passes close and you think she may have been hunted, look to see if her feet are dirty. Watch her carefully till she is out of sight and make a mental note of the exact spot you saw her last. This is very important, and like marking a falling golf ball, not very easy to accomplish, but it will save much time if you are able to point out the exact spot. A hare may be running in a certain direction when you last saw her and you imagine she will continue to follow that course, but in all probability when out of sight will double.

Therefore in giving information to the huntsman, point to the spot where you last saw her and not to where you thought she was going. However, in your first few days it is better to keep your eyes open and your mouth shut, observing carefully all that happens, as unless accustomed to seeing the two animals you might mistake a rabbit for a hare.

When possible run on the down-wind side of the pack, but always keep behind, giving it plenty of room to swing, as a hare is liable to jink or turn at any moment. Should you perchance have your feet in the exact place the hare has run, you are, of course, in the wrong, but it will only make matters worse to move, therefore stand perfectly still with your head turned in the direction the hare has gone. Remember your scent—two baths a day notwithstanding—is much stronger than the hare's and the more you move the stronger it becomes.

When you have attained some knowledge of the sport you may often be able to render assistance to the huntsman by viewing a tired hare, and in other matters which increase your interest in a day's hunting.

Fresh air and exercise are two of the benefits to be reaped by following beagles, but the novice would add considerably to his pleasure if he would read some hunting literature and learn the rudiments of venerie. When hounds are running fast and you are able to keep up with them it is a delightful sensation that cannot be equalled, but when it comes to slow hunting, anyone taking the trouble to watch the pack at work cannot fail to be interested. Hares when once a little way ahead of hounds are full of artful dodges and hunting is then seen at its best, a time also when the indifferent runner can get near enough to see.

THE FIELD

SYMPATHY WITH THE HOUND

In hunting, whether it be of fox or hare, every follower should identify himself with hounds' aims and give his entire sympathy to them. If he allows himself to sympathise with the hare, his pleasure in the chase will be neutralised and he might as well go home at once.

INDEX

Appetite, 97
Aspect of Kennels, 86
Association, Masters of,
    Harriers and Beagles, 156

Babblers, 69
Backs, 36
Balance, 67
Beagles, College and School
    Packs, 156
Benger's Food, 122
Bicol, 104
    Bitches, dosing of, 79
Blood, out of, 165
Breeding, 49, 64
Buying of hounds, 40

Cabbages, 104
Calomel, 121
Casting, 171, 173
Character, 38
Chorea, 121
Clapham's Foxes, Foxhounds
    and Foxhunting, 35
Cleanliness, 124
Cod liver oil, 104
Colour, 27, 75

Committee, hunt, 158
Concrete, 88, 90
Condition, 98
Constitution, 65
Cooking food, 92
Counting Hounds, 185
Country, 152
Couples, breaking with, 58
Courage, 27, 76

Dainty feeders, 98
Damaging property, 188, 209
Dew-claws, cutting of, 55
Diet, change of, 92
Dipping, 105
Discipline, 99, 102
Diseases, 116
Distemper, 116
Distemper research, 125
Dosing of Bitches, 79
Down wind running, 216
Dress, 204
Dressing, 105
Dressing mixture, 106
Dressing whelps, 55
Drive, 71

Earmite, 105

INDEX

Eczema, 105
Education of young hounds, 197
Elbows, 29
Exercise, 98
Expression, 38
  time of, 100
  fast, 101

Farmers, consideration of, 155, 188, 210
Fat hounds, 47
Feeding, 91
  biscuit, 96
  time of, 96, 97
Feet, 33
Female tap root, 73
Fens, hunting in, 21
Field, 200
Fitness of followers, 211
Fixture cards, 203
Flesh, raw, 95
Food, temperature of, 92
Footwear, importance of, 206
Fox, 17, 187
Fox covers, 187

Gates, closing of, 209
Grass run, 53, 80, 86, 118

Halloos, 163
Hare, 134
  pugnacity of, 135
  inherited instincts of, 137
  turning down, 144
  breeding, 145

Hares and Rabbits Bill, 18
Heading and tailing of pack, 23
Height of Hounds, 21
Hocks, 32
Hounds' hearing, 194
Human scent, 213
Huntsman, 161
  interference with, 161
  professional, 163
Hysteria, 127
  after effects, 131

Inbreeding, 73
Increasing number of packs, 157

Jaundice, 121
Jeyes' Fluid, 105, 123, 129

Keepers, 141, 176
Kennel book, 60
Kennel lameness, 83, 86
Kennelman, 110
  disposition, 111
  experience necessary, 111
  wages of, 113
Kennels, ventilation of, 81
  material, 83
  plan of, 84
  ground plan, 87
  aspect of, 88
Kill, 167
Knees, 30

Lambs, 99

INDEX

Lameness, kennel, 83
Landowners, 152
Legs, 29
Leicester sale, 41
Level running, 42
Leverets, 146
Lifting, 171
Litters, feeding of, 51
Loins, 31
Looks, 26
Loyalty of Whips, 196

Market gardens, 210
Marking whelps, 59
Masters of Foxhounds, 153
Medicine, 103, 119
Methods of hunting, 164
Muteness, 71

Naming a pack, 159
Necks, 29
Neighbouring hunts, 152
Nettles, 104
Noisy whips, 194
Non-changing instincts, 196
Nose, 37

Oatmeal, 91
Overcrowding, 89
Ownership of hounds, 157

Pedigree, 77
Perseverance in hunting, 181
Peterborough, 27, 44
Pheasants, 188
Pneumonia, 120

Prizes, 62
Punishment, 190, 193
Puppy shows, 62

Quality, 68, 76
Quarters, 31

Rabbits, 145
Rating of hounds, 192
Ribs, 34
Rice, 93
Riot, 190
Roads, hares running, 150, 176
Rules for followers, 214

Scent, changing with tired hare, 164, 182
Scratch packs, 155
Sheep, 82, 150
Sheep·stain, 169
   chasing of, 187, 193
Shooting tenants, 154, 188
Shoulders, 29
Showing, 45
Skirters, 69
Smeuses, 138
Speed of hounds, 24
Stallion hounds, 66
Stamina, 27, 65, 68
Sticky going, 21
Stoat, 179
Stockholm tar, 120
Subscriptions, 201
Sympathy with hounds, 217

INDEX

Tongue, 69

Uniform, 205

Ventilation, 86
Vermifuges, 107
Viewing hare, 180

Walks, 56, 61
Whelping, 49

Whelps, best time for birth, 78
Whip cracking, 189
Whipper-in, 187
Whips, carrying of, 184
Worm pills, 107
Worms, 57, 79, 108, 118

Yellows, 121
Young hounds, 56, 58, 197